LATIN

GRAMMAR

ROBERT J. HENLE, S.J.

LOYOLAPRESS.

CHICAGO

LOYOLA PRESS.
www.loyolapress.com

© 1958
Copyright 1945

Library of Congress Catalog Card Number: 58-10997

ISBN-13: 978-0-8294-0112-7
ISBN-10: 0-8294-0112-1

Printed in the United States of America.
22 23 24 25 26 27 28 29 30 31 LSC 36 35 34 33 32 31 30 29 28 27

CONTENTS

PART 1
FORMS

PART 2
SYNTAX

PART 1

FORMS

INTRODUCTORY

1   **The Alphabet.** The Latin alphabet has no **w** or **y**; otherwise it is the same as the English.

Pronunciation.[1] The Latin letters are pronounced as follows:

2   **Vowels:** *Long*

Long	*Short*
ā as in *father;*	**a** as in *facility;*
ē as in *they;*	**e** as in *get;*
ī as in *machine;*	**i** as in *fit;*
ō as in *no;*	**o** as in *obey;*
ū as in *rule.*	**u** as in *put.*

3   **Note:** Very often in practice the difference between the long and short vowels is ignored, all of them being given the quality of long vowels. In reading poetry a quantitative difference alone is then maintained between long and short vowels.

4   **Diphthongs:**

ae
oe   } like *e* in *they;*

au   like *ou* in *out.*

5   **Consonants:**

Most of the consonants are pronounced as in English, but **c** and **g** are soft before **e, i, ae, oe;** otherwise hard.

Hard **c** as in *cat;* soft **c** as in *cell.*

Hard **g** as in *gun;* soft **g** as in *germ.*

j is pronounced like **y** as in *yet.*

---

[1]For the Roman and Italian systems see Nos. 1018-19. The system here given is called the Continental or Traditional System.

1

Division into Syllables.

6 a. A single consonant goes with the following vowel.

    mā/ter; nau/ta; nō/men

7 b. Two or more consonants are divided after the first.

    por/ta; exer/citus; pul/chra

8 Note: But when a mute (c, g, p, b, t, d) or f is followed by r or l, both consonants go with the following vowel.

    la/crima; a/grum; pa/trem; va/fra; locu/plēs

Accent.

9 a. In words of two syllables the accent is on the first.

    vía; béllum

10 b. In words of more than two syllables, if the second last syllable is long it is accented; otherwise the accent is on the third last syllable.

    vidérunt; ágmĭne

Quantity of Syllables.

11 a. A syllable is short if it contains a vowel that is short by nature or that is followed by another vowel or diphthong.

    regĕre; glorĭa

12 b. A syllable is long if it contains a vowel that is long by nature[1] or a vowel that is followed by two consonants other than a mute (c, g, p, b, t, d) or f followed by a liquid (r, l).

    studēre; regendus

13 Note: x and z each count as two consonants (cs and ds); h and the u in qu do not count as consonants.

---

[1] In this GRAMMAR and in its companion volumes all vowels *long by nature* are marked, as: *studēre*. Otherwise they are unmarked.

NOUNS

14   **Nouns** have gender, number, case, and declension.

15   **Gender.** There are three genders in Latin: masculine, feminine, neuter.

16   All nouns meaning individual male persons are masculine.

17   All nouns meaning individual female persons are feminine.

18   The gender of other nouns must be learned from their declension or from the vocabularies.

19   **Number.** There are two numbers in Latin: singular and plural.

20   The singular speaks of one: **via,** *a road.*

21   The plural speaks of more than one: **viae,** *roads.*

22   **Case.** There are six cases in Latin:

Nominative:	the case of the **Subject.**
Genitive:	the case of the **Possessor.**
Dative:	the case of the **Indirect Object;** the 'to' or 'for' case.
Accusative:	the case of the **Direct Object.**
Ablative:	the 'by-with-from' case [used *frequently* with prepositions].
Vocative:	the case of the **Person Addressed.**

23   **Declension.** Declension consists in adding the proper ENDINGS to the STEM to show the different genders, numbers, and cases.

24   **Stem.** The stem is found by dropping the ENDING of the GENITIVE SINGULAR.

      vi-ae, *stem:* **vi-**

3

25   **The Five Declensions.** There are five declensions in Latin. They can be distinguished by the endings of the genitive singular.

1	2	3	4	5
-ae	-ī	-is	-ūs	-eī
vi-ae	serv-ī	lēg-is	port-ūs	r-eī

26   **How to Decline a Noun.** The nominative, genitive, and gender of a noun determine which model it follows. Add the endings of that model to the stem.

Note:

27   a. The **stem** is that part of the word which remains the same in spelling throughout the declension. It gives the **meaning** of the word. The **endings** show **what the word does in the sentence,** whether it is the subject, direct object, indirect object, *etc.*

28   b. The vocative of all nouns and adjectives is always like the nominative except in singular nouns in **-us** of the second declension: these have **-e. Serv-e!** *Slave!* **Exceptions:** Proper nouns in **-ius** and **fīlius,** *son,* have only **-ī** in the vocative singular. **Vergilius,** voc. **Vergilī; fīlius,** voc. **fīlī.** The vocative singular of **Deus,** *God,* is **Deus;** the vocative masculine singular of **meus** is **mī; fīlī mī!** *my son!*

29   c. The accusative of neuter nouns and adjectives is always like the nominative.

30   d. Names of towns, and **domus,** *home,* and **rūs,** *country,* have another case—the locative—expressing place where. In singulars of the first and second declensions the locative is like the genitive: **Rōmae,** *at Rome.* In all others it is like the ablative: **Carthāgine (Carthāgō, Carthāginis),** *at Carthage.* But **rūs,** *country,* has **rūrī** or **rūre,** *in the country.* See No. 915.

31   The First Declension.

		Form	Meaning	Use
	Nom.	terr-a	land, the (a)[1] land	subject
	Gen.	terr-ae	of the (a) land	possessive
S.	Dat.	terr-ae	to or for the (a) land	indirect object
	Acc.	terr-am	the (a) land	direct object
	Abl.	terr-ā	by, with, from the (a) land	

	Nom.	terr-ae	lands, the lands	subject
	Gen.	terr-ārum	of the lands	possessive
P.	Dat.	terr-īs	to or for the lands	indirect object
	Acc.	terr-ās	lands, the lands	direct object
	Abl.	terr-īs	by, with, from the lands	

Gender:[2]

32   a. All nouns naming individual male persons are masculine.

nauta, ae, *a sailor*, masculine. (*Sailors are usually men.*)

33   b. All others are feminine.

terra, ae, *land,* feminine.

---

[1]There is no article, definite *(the)* or indefinite *(a, an)* in Latin. *Terra,* therefore, translates 'land,' 'a land,' 'the land.'

[2]No gender will be indicated in the vocabularies for nouns following the rules given in the GRAMMAR; all others will have their gender indicated and should be so learned.

34　　　**Masculine Nouns of the Second Declension.**

		Form	*Meaning*	*Use*
	Nom.	serv-us	*the slave*[1]	*subject*
	Gen.	serv-ī[2]	*of the slave, the slave's*	*possessive*
S.	*Dat.*	serv-ō	*to or for the slave*	*indirect object*
	Acc.	serv-um	*the slave*	*direct object*
	Abl.	serv-ō	*by, with, from the slave*	
	Nom.	serv-ī	*the slaves*	*subject*
	Gen.	serv-ōrum	*of the slaves, the slaves'*	*possessive*
P.	*Dat.*	serv-īs	*to or for the slaves*	*indirect object*
	Acc.	serv-ōs	*the slaves*	*direct object*
	Abl.	serv-īs	*by, with, from the slaves*	

35　　　**Gender:** Generally masculine.

36　　　**Note:** Proper names in **-ius** and **fīlius**, *son,* form their vocative singular in **-ī. Vergilius, Vergilī; fīlius, fīlī.**

---

[1]*Servus*, of course, may be translated either 'slave,' 'the slave,' or 'a slave.'
[2]Nouns in *-ius* and *-ium* more properly have *ī* in the genitive in place of *iī* (as *fīlius*, gen. *fīlī*; *ingenium*, gen. *ingenī*) but in the first two years of this course the full form in *iī* will be used. The accent in the contracted form remains where it was in the uncontracted form: *ingéniī, ingénī*.

37   **Neuter Nouns of the Second Declension.**

		Form	Meaning	Use
	Nom.	bell-um	*the war*[1]	*subject*
	Gen.	bell-ī	*of the war*	*possessive*
S.	*Dat.*	bell-ō	*to or for the war*	*indirect object*
	Acc.	bell-um	*the war*	*direct object*
	Abl.	bell-ō	*by, with, from the war*	
	Nom.	bell-a	*the wars*	*subject*
	Gen.	bell-ōrum	*of the wars*	*possessive*
P.	*Dat.*	bell-īs	*to or for the wars*	*indirect object*
	Acc.	bell-a	*the wars*	*direct object*
	Abl.	bell-īs	*by, with, from the wars*	

38   **Gender:** All neuter.[2]

39   **Note:** The accusative is like the nominative in all neuter
nouns and adjectives. Thus, singular nom. **bellum**,
acc. **bellum**; plural nom. **bella**, acc. **bella**. (Cf.
flūmen, No. 64, **gravis, e**, No. 78, *etc.*)

---

[1] *Bellum*, of course, may be translated 'war,' 'the war,' or 'a war.'
[2] There are no exceptions.

40   Vir, virī, *man*, and words like **ager, agrī,** *field,* and **puer, puerī,** *boy,* belong to the second declension. (Note the genitive in -ī.) They are declined like **servus** except in the nominative (and vocative) singular. Thus:

41	vir	**42**	ager	**43**	puer
	vir-ī		agr-ī		puer-ī
	vir-ō		agr-ō		puer-ō
	vir-um		agr-um		puer-um
	vir-ō		agr-ō		puer-ō
	vir-ī		agr-ī		puer-ī
	vir-ōrum		agr-ōrum		puer-ōrum
	vir-īs		agr-īs		puer-īs
	vir-ōs		agr-ōs		puer-ōs
	vir-īs		agr-īs		puer-īs

44   Deus, ī, *God,* shows peculiarities in the underlined forms. The vocative singular is **Deus.**

	Sing.	*Plural*
Nom.	deus	d̲ī̲ (deī, d̲iī̲)[1]
Gen.	deī	deōrum (d̲eūm̲)
Dat.	deō	d̲ī̲s̲ (deīs, d̲iīs̲)
Acc.	deum	deōs
Abl.	deō	d̲ī̲s̲ (deīs, d̲iīs̲)

---

[1] The forms in parentheses occur in some writers.

45   **The Third Declension.** The nominative singular of the third declension has no model ending. Thus **lēx,** *law,* **pars,** *part,* **flūmen,** *river,* **hostis,** *enemy,* are all nouns of the third declension. The genitive ending (for the third declension, always **-is**) shows the declension and gives the stem.

Gender:[1]

46   Nouns naming individual male persons are masculine:

     mīles, mīlitis, *m., soldier*

47   Nouns naming individual female persons are feminine:

     māter, mātris, *f., mother*

48   **Note:** These two rules (Nos. 46, 47) should always be applied before Nos. 49 to 52. Thus **mīles** would be feminine by the SOX rule (No. 50), but rule No. 46 is applied first, hence **mīles** is masculine.

49   Nouns ending in **-er, -or (ERROR)** are masculine.

50   Nouns ending in **-s, -o, -x (SOX)** are feminine.

51   Nouns ending in **-l, -a, -n, -c, -e, -t (LANCET)** are neuter.

52   **Note:** But masculinī generis

     are words in **-os, -nis, -guis,** and **-cis,**

     in **-es (-itis)** and **-ex (-icis);**

     as neuter mark the **-us** (with **-ris**).

53   **Declension.** First find the gender of the noun. Then find the stem from the genitive.

54   For masculine and feminine nouns, add the endings of **lēx** or **pars** according to the rules in Nos. 59-63.

55   For neuter nouns add the endings of **flūmen.**[2]

56   The vocative is always like the nominative.

---

[1]When the gender of nouns follows rules Nos. 44 to 51, no gender will be given in the companion volumes; thus, *pars, partis* (sox). When nouns follow rule No. 52 or are altogether exceptional the gender will be given, thus, *tempus, temporis, n.*

[2]For the few exceptions see the footnote on No. 64.

Masculine and Feminine Nouns of the Third Declension.

		57			**58**	
	Nom.	lēx	*the law*	pars	*the part*
	Gen.	lēg-is	*of the law*	part-is	*of the part*
S.	*Dat.*	lēg-ī	*to (for) the law*	part-ī	*to (for) the part*
	Acc.	lēg-em	*the law*	part-em	*the part*
	Abl.	lēg-e	*by, etc., the law*	part-e	*by, etc., the part*
	Nom.	lēg-ēs	*the laws*	part-ēs	*the parts*
	Gen.	lēg-um	*of the laws*	part-ium	*of the parts*
P.	*Dat.*	lēg-ibus	*to (for) the laws*	part-ibus	*to (for) the parts*
	Acc.	lēg-ēs	*the laws*	part-ēs	*the parts*
	Abl.	lēg-ibus	*by, etc., the laws*	part-ibus	*by, etc., the parts*

59   Note: All masculine and feminine nouns of the third declension are declined like **lēx** except the following nouns which have **-ium** in the genitive plural like **part-ium**:

60   1. Nouns that have the same number of syllables in the genitive singular as in the nominative singular, as: **hostis, hostis (host-ium),** *enemy.*

61   2. Nouns whose stem ends in two consonants, as: **gēns, gentis,** *tribe,* stem, **gent-,** hence **gentium.**

Exceptions:

62   a. With **-um** instead of **-ium: senum, patrum, mēnsum, mātrum, canum, juvenum,** and **frātrum.**[1]

63   b. With **-ium** instead of **-um: vīrium, lītium, faucium, Penātium, imbrium** and **nivium, Samnītium, optimātium.**[2]

---

[1] of old men, fathers, months and mothers, of dogs and youths, and brothers.
[2] of strength and quarrels, of jaws and household gods, of rains and snows, of Samnites and aristocrats.

64   Neuter Nouns of the Third Declension.

	Nom.	flūmen[1]	the river
	Gen.	flūmin-is	of the river
S.	Dat.	flūmin-ī	to or for the river
	Acc.	flūmen	the river
	Abl.	flūmin-e	by, with, from the river
	Nom.	flūmin-a	the rivers
	Gen.	flūmin-um	of the rivers
P.	Dat.	flūmin-ibus	to or for the rivers
	Acc.	flūmin-a	the rivers
	Abl.	flūmin-ibus	by, with, from the rivers

---

[1]All neuter nouns of the third declension are declined like *flūmen* except
the very few which end their nominative with *-e, -al, -ar*. These have *-ī*
in the ablative singular, *-ia* in the nominative and accusative, plural, and
-ium in the genitive plural. Thus *mare, maris* has ablative singular *mar-ī*,
nominative and accusative plural *mar-ia*, and genitive plural *mar-ium*.

65   The Fourth Declension.

S.	*Nom.*	port-us	*the harbor*
	Gen.	port-ūs	*of the harbor*
	Dat.	port-uī	*to or for the harbor*
	Acc.	port-um	*the harbor*
	Abl.	port-ū	*by, with, from the harbor*

P.	*Nom.*	port-ūs	*the harbors*
	Gen.	port-uum	*of the harbors*
	Dat.	port-ibus	*to or for the harbors*
	Acc.	port-ūs	*the harbors*
	Abl.	port-ibus	*by, with, from the harbors*

66   Gender: All masculine except **manus, ūs,** *f., hand,* **domus, ūs,** *f., house,* **cornū, ūs,** *n., horn,* **genū, ūs,** *n., knee,* and a few others.

67   **Domus, ūs,** *f., house, home,* shows peculiarities in the under-lined forms. The locative is **domī,** *at home* (Nos. 30, 915).

	Sing.	*Plural*
Nom.	domus	domūs
Gen.	domūs	domōrum or domuum
Dat.	domuī	domibus
Acc.	domum	domōs or domūs
Abl.	domō	domibus

68   Neuter nouns of the fourth declension have **-ū** in the accusative singular (like the nominative) and **-ua** in the nominative and accusative plural.

	Sing.	*Plural*
Nom.	corn-ū	corn-ua
Gen.	corn-ūs	corn-uum
Dat.	corn-ū	corn-ibus
Acc.	corn-ū	corn-ua
Abl.	corn-ū	corn-ibus

69 The Fifth Declension.

S.	*Nom.*	rēs	*the thing*
	Gen.	r-eī	*of the thing*
	Dat.	r-eī	*to or for the thing*
	Acc.	r-em	*the thing*
	Abl.	r-ē	*by, with, from the thing*
P.	*Nom.*	r-ēs	*the things*
	Gen.	r-ērum	*of the things*
	Dat.	r-ēbus	*to or for the things*
	Acc.	r-ēs	*the things*
	Abl.	r-ēbus	*by, with, from the things*

70 **Gender:** All feminine except **diēs, diēī** which is generally masculine. In the singular, however, when it means a set date or a "period of time" even **diēs** is often feminine. Certain nouns, such as **fidēs,** *f., faith,* have no plural forms.

71 **Note:** The genitive and dative singular ending of the fifth declension is **ēī** instead of **eī** when the stem ends in a vowel, as **diēs,** stem, **di,** therefore **di-ēī.**

ADJECTIVES

72   **Adjectives in -us of the First and Second Declensions.**

		Masc. like *servus*	*Fem.* like *porta*	*Neut.* like *bellum*
S.	*Nom.*	magn-us	magn-a	magn-um
	Gen.	magn-ī	magn-ae	magn-ī
	Dat.	magn-ō	magn-ae	magn-ō
	Acc.	magn-um	magn-am	magn-um
	Abl.	magn-ō	magn-ā	magn-ō
P.	*Nom.*	magn-ī	magn-ae	magn-a
	Gen.	magn-ōrum	magn-ārum	magn-ōrum
	Dat.	magn-īs	magn-īs	magn-īs
	Acc.	magn-ōs	magn-ās	magn-a
	Abl.	magn-īs	magn-īs	magn-īs

73   **How to Decline an Adjective.**

1. Learn the nominative and genitive[1] from the vocabularies.

2. These show what model the adjective follows.

3. Add the endings of this model to the stem.

---

[1]The genitive of adjectives is not given in vocabularies when it is clear from the nominative, as *magnus, a, um* (stem, *magn-*).

74 **Adjectives in -er of the First and Second Declensions.**

There are two other kinds of adjectives in the first and second declensions:

miser, miser-a, miser-um (stem, **miser-**), *wretched*

integer, integr-a, integr-um (stem, **integr-**), *fresh*

These adjectives have the same endings as **magnus** except in the nominative singular masculine (**miser, integer**).

		Masc. like *puer*	*Fem.* like *porta*	*Neut.* like *bellum*
75				
	Nom.	MISER	miser-a	miser-um
	Gen.	miser-ī	miser-ae	miser-ī
S.	Dat.	miser-ō	miser-ae	miser-ō
	Acc.	miser-um	miser-am	miser-um
	Abl.	miser-ō	miser-ā	miser-ō
	Nom.	miser-ī	miser-ae	miser-a
	Gen.	miser-ōrum	miser-ārum	miser-ōrum
P.	Dat.	miser-īs	miser-īs	miser-īs
	Acc.	miser-ōs	miser-ās	miser-a
	Abl.	miser-īs	miser-īs	miser-īs

		Masc. like *ager*	*Fem.* like *porta*	*Neut.* like *bellum*
76				
	Nom.	INTEGER	integr-a	integr-um
	Gen.	integr-ī	integr-ae	integr-ī
S.	Dat.	integr-ō	integr-ae	integr-ō
	Acc.	integr-um	integr-am	integr-um
	Abl.	integr-ō	integr-ā	integr-ō
	Nom.	integr-ī	integr-ae	integr-a
	Gen.	integr-ōrum	integr-ārum	integr-ōrum
P.	Dat.	integr-īs	integr-īs	integr-īs
	Acc.	integr-ōs	integr-ās	integr-a
	Abl.	integr-īs	integr-īs	integr-īs

77   **Adjectives in -*is*, -*is*, -*e* of the Third Declension.**

The most important kind of adjectives in the third declension has -is, -is, -e in the nominative.

Gravis, e,[1] *heavy, severe, serious,* is declined thus:

78

		Masc.	*Fem.*	*Neut.*
	Nom.	grav-is	grav-is	grav-e
	Gen.	grav-is	grav-is	grav-is
S.	*Dat.*	grav-ī	grav-ī	grav-ī
	Acc.	grav-em	grav-em	grav-e
	Abl.	grav-ī	grav-ī	grav-ī
	Nom.	grav-ēs	grav-ēs	grav-ia
	Gen.	grav-ium	grav-ium	grav-ium
P.	*Dat.*	grav-ibus	grav-ibus	grav-ibus
	Acc.	grav-ēs	grav-ēs	grav-ia
	Abl.	grav-ibus	grav-ibus	grav-ibus

79   **Third Declension Adjectives of Three Endings.**

ācer, ācris, ācre,[2] *sharp, keen, eager*   (stem, ācr-),

celer, celeris, celere,[2] *swift*   (stem, celer-).

These are declined like **gravis, e,** except in *one* case—the nominative singular masculine (ācer, celer). Therefore:

a. Find the stem from the feminine, thus:

ācris; stem, ācr-; celeris; stem, celer-.

b. Add the endings of **gravis, e.**

-----

[1] Adjectives of this kind will be given in the vocabularies thus: *gravis, e,* since the stem *(grav-)* is clear from the nominative.

[2] Adjectives of this class will always be given in the vocabularies thus: *ācer, ācris, ācre.* The stem can be derived from the feminine: *ācris;* stem, *ācr-.*

		Masc.	*Fem.*	*Neut.*
80				
	Nom.	ĀCER	ācr-is	ācr-e
	Gen.	ācr-is	ācr-is	ācr-is
S.	*Dat.*	ācr-ī	ācr-ī	ācr-ī
	Acc.	ācr-em	ācr-em	ācr-e
	Abl.	ācr-ī	ācr-ī	ācr-ī
	Nom.	ācr-ēs	ācr-ēs	ācr-ia
	Gen.	ācr-ium	ācr-ium	ācr-ium
P.	*Dat.*	ācr-ibus	ācr-ibus	ācr-ibus
	Acc.	ācr-ēs	ācr-ēs	ācr-ia
	Abl.	ācr-ibus	ācr-ibus	ācr-ibus

81   **Third Declension Adjectives of One Ending.**

dīligēns (*gen.* dīligentis)[1]   stem: dīligent-

pār (*gen.* paris)[1]   stem: par-

audāx (*gen.* audācis)[1]   stem: audāc-

praeceps (*gen.* praecipitis)[1]   stem: praecipit-

These adjectives are all declined like **gravis, e,** except in the nominative singular (which is the same in all three genders) and in the accusative singular neuter (which is always like the nominative).

		Masc.	*Fem.*	*Neut.*
82				
	Nom.	**DĪLIGĒNS**	**DĪLIGĒNS**	**DĪLIGĒNS**
	Gen.	dīligent-is	dīligent-is	dīligent-is
S.	*Dat.*	dīligent-ī	dīligent-ī	dīligent-ī
	Acc.	dīligent-em	dīligent-em	**DĪLIGĒNS**
	Abl.	dīligent-ī	dīligent-ī	dīligent-ī
	Nom.	dīligent-ēs	dīligent-ēs	dīligent-ia
	Gen.	dīligent-ium	dīligent-ium	dīligent-ium
P.	*Dat.*	dīligent-ibus	dīligent-ibus	dīligent-ibus
	Acc.	dīligent-ēs	dīligent-ēs	dīligent-ia
	Abl.	dīligent-ibus	dīligent-ibus	dīligent-ibus

---

[1]Adjectives of this class will always be given in the vocabularies **thus:** *dīligēns* (gen. *dīligentis*).

83   Vetus (*gen.* veteris), *old,* is declined like **lēx** and **flūmen.**

		Masc. like *lēx*	*Fem.* like *lēx*	*Neut.* like *flūmen*
S.	*Nom.*	**VETUS**	**VETUS**	**VETUS**
	Gen.	veter-is	veter-is	veter-is
	Dat.	veter-ī	veter-ī	veter-ī
	Acc.	veter-em	veter-em	vetus
	Abl.	veter-e	vetèr-e	veter-e
P.	*Nom.*	veter-ēs	veter-ēs	veter-a
	Gen.	veter-um	veter-um	veter-um
	Dat.	veter-ibus	veter-ibus	veter-ibus
	Acc.	veter-ēs	veter-ēs	veter-a
	Abl.	veter-ibus	veter-ibus	veter-ibus

Irregular Adjectives.

84   a. The following adjectives are declined like **ūnus, a, um**
(No. 114) in the singular and like **magnī, ae, a** in the
plural:

> **sōlus, a, um,** *alone*
>
> **tōtus, a, um,** *whole*
>
> **ūllus, a, um,** *any (at all)*
>
> **nūllus, a, um,** *no, not any*

Thus:	*Nom.*	sōlus	sōla	sōlum
	Gen.	sōlīus	sōlīus	sōlīus
	Dat.	sōlī	sōlī	sōlī
	Acc.	sōlum	*etc.*	

85 b. **Alius, alia, aliud,** *other, another,* is regular except in the underlined forms:

	Nom.	alius	alia	aliud
	Gen.	alīus	alīus	alīus
S.	*Dat.*	aliī	aliī	aliī
	Acc.	alium	aliam	aliud
	Abl.	aliō	aliā	aliō

P.	*Nom.*	ali-ī	ali-ae	ali-a

etc. (like **magnī, ae, a**)

86 Note: The genitive singular **alīus** is rarely used. The genitive singular of **alter, alterīus,** or the adjective **aliēnus, a, um,** *belonging to another,* is used instead.

87 c. **Alter, altera, alterum,** *the other, one (of two),* or *the second,* is regular (like **miser**) except in the genitive and dative singular:

	Nom.	alter	altera	alterum
	Gen.	alter-īus	alter-īus	alter-īus
S.	*Dat.*	alter-ī	alter-ī	alter-ī
	Acc.	alter-um	alter-am	alter-um
		etc.		

88 d. **Neuter, neutra, neutrum,** *neither (of two),* and the interrogative **uter, utra, utrum,** *which (of two),* are declined like **alter, altera, alterum.**

Comparison of Adjectives.

89   The comparative of adjectives in English is formed either by using the adverb 'more' or by adding -*er* to the adjective.

90   The superlative of adjectives in English is formed either by using the adverb 'most' or by adding -*est* to the adjective:

Positive	Comparative	Superlative
certain	more certain	most certain
heavy	heavier	heaviest

In Latin:

91   To form the COMPARATIVE add **-ior, -ius** to the STEM of the positive.

92   To form the SUPERLATIVE add **-issimus, -issima, -issimum** to the STEM of the positive.

Positive	Comparative	Superlative
cert-us	certior, certius	certissimus, a, um
certain	*more certain*	*most certain*
grav-is	gravior, gravius	gravissimus, a, um
heavy	*heavier*	*heaviest*
dīligēns stem: **dīligent-**	dīligentior, dīligentius	dīligentissimus, a, um
careful	*more careful*	*most careful*
audāx stem: **audāc-**	audācior, audācius	audācissimus, a, um
daring	*more daring*	*most daring*

93   The Latin comparative and superlative are weaker than the English (Nos. 854, 856) and are frequently translated by the adverbs 'rather' (comparative) and 'very' (superlative) with the positive of the adjective.

certior, certius	*rather certain*
certissimus, a, um	*very certain*

Note:

94   a. Adjectives in **-er** add **-rimus** to the NOMINATIVE MASCULINE SINGULAR to form the SUPERLATIVE.

Positive	*Superlative*
miser, misera, miserum	**miserrimus, a, um**
wretched	*most wretched*
ācer, ācris, ācre	**ācerrimus, a, um**
sharp	*sharpest*

95   **Note:** But the COMPARATIVES of these words follow the regular rule, No. 91. Thus:

stem: **miser-**   comp.: **miserior, miserius**
stem: **ācr-**   comp.: **ācrior, ācrius**

96   b. **Similis,** *like,* **dissimilis,** *unlike,* **facilis,** *easy,* **humilis,** *low,* **difficilis,** *difficult,* **gracilis,** *graceful,* add **-limus** to the stem to form the SUPERLATIVE.

Positive	*Superlative*
facilis, e	**facillimus, a, um**
stem: **facil-**	
easy	*easiest*

97   **Note:** But the comparatives of these words follow the regular rule, No. 91. Thus:

stem: **facil-**   **comp.: facilior, facilius**

98   c. Adjectives ending in **-us** preceded by a vowel (except **qu** or **gu**) form their comparative and superlative with the adverbs **magis** and **maximē**.

Positive:	*doubtful*	**dubius, a, um**
Comparative:	*more doubtful*	**magis dubius, a, um**
Superlative:	*most doubtful*	**maximē dubius, a, um**

99 Irregular Comparatives and Superlatives.[1]

1. **bonus,** *good*	**mel-ior, -ius,** *better*	**optimus,** *best*
2. **malus,** *bad*	**pējor, pējus,** *worse*	**pessimus,** *worst*
3. **magnus,** *great*	**mājor, mājus,** *greater*	**maximus,** *greatest*
4. **parvus,** *small*	**min-or, -us,** *smaller*	**minimus,** *smallest*
5. **multus,** *much*	**plūs** (n.),[2] *more*	**plūrimus,** *most*
6. **multī,** *many*	**plūr-ēs, -a,**[2] *more*	**plūrimī,** *very many*
7. **juvenis,** *young*	**jun-ior, ius,** *younger*	[**nātū minimus,** *youngest*]
8. **senex,** *aged*	**sen-ior, ius,** *elder*	[**nātū maximus,** *eldest*]
9. **novus,** *new*	[**recent-ior, -ius,** *fresher*]	**novissimus,** *last*
10. **vetus (veter-),** *old*	[**vetust-ior, -ius,** *older*]	**veterrimus,** *oldest*
11. **propinquus,** *near*	**prop-ior, -ius,** *nearer*	**proximus,** *nearest, next*

---

[1]In this list only the masculine of the positive and superlative degrees are given. The feminine and neuter are formed regularly.

[2]*Plūs* is a noun in the singular: Nom. *plūs,* Gen. *plūris,* Dat. ——, Acc. *plūs,* Abl. *plūre; plūs vinī,* 'more wine' (lit. 'more of wine'). In the plural it is an adjective: *plūrēs, plūrēs, plūra, plūrium, etc.*

100   In the cases of the following comparatives and superlatives the corresponding positive adjective does not exist, or is rare :[1]

1. dēterior, *worse*   dēterrimus, *worst*

2. exterior, *outer*   extrēmus, *outermost*

3. īnferior, *lower*   īmus } *lowest*
                      īnfimus

4. interior, *inner*   intimus, *inmost*

5. posterior, *later*   postrēmus, *last*

6. prior, *former*   prīmus, *first*

7. superior, *higher*   suprēmus } *highest*
                      summus

8. ulterior, *farther*   ultimus, *farthest*

---

[1]In this list only the masculine is given; the feminine and neuter are formed regularly.

Declension of Comparatives and Superlatives.

101 All COMPARATIVES are declined like **lēx** and **flūmen**. The STEM is always the full MASCULINE SINGULAR NOMINATIVE, thus: stem: **GRAVIOR-**.

		Masc. like *lēx*	*Fem.* like *lēx*	*Neut.* like *flūmen*
	Nom.	gravior	gravior	gravius
	Gen.	graviōr-is	graviōr-is	graviōr-is
S.	*Dat.*	graviōr-ī	graviōr-ī	graviōr-ī
	Acc.	graviōr-em	graviōr-em	gravius
	Abl.	graviōr-e	graviōr-e	graviōr-e
	Nom.	graviōr-ēs	graviōr-ēs	graviōr-a
	Gen.	graviōr-um	graviōr-um	graviōr-um
P.	*Dat.*	graviōr-ibus	graviōr-ibus	graviōr-ibus
	Acc.	graviōr-ēs	graviōr-ēs	graviōr-a
	Abl.	graviōr-ibus	graviōr-ibus	graviōr-ibus

102 All SUPERLATIVES are declined like **magnus, a, um**. Thus:

certissim-us	certissim-a	certissim-um
certissim-ī	certissim-ae	certissim-ī
etc.		

ADVERBS

103 **Formation of Adverbs.** Although there are many other kinds of adverbs in Latin, a large number are formed from adjectives. The following GENERAL RULES may be given:

104 a. To form adverbs from adjectives of the **first** and **second** declensions, add **-ē** to the STEM:

Adjective	Stem	Adverb
lātus, a, um	**lāt-**	**lātē**
wide		*widely*
līber, lībera, līberum	**līber-**	**līberē**
free		*freely*

105 **Note:** But some adverbs have **-ō** instead of **-ē**:

Adjective	Stem	Adverb
tūtus, a, um	**tūt-**	**tūtō**
safe		*safely*

106 b. To form adverbs from adjectives of the **third** declension, add **-iter** to the STEM:

Adjective	Stem	Adverb
gravis, e	**grav-**	**graviter**
serious		*seriously*
ācer, ācris, ācre	**ācr-**	**ācriter**
sharp		*sharply*

107 **Note:** But for adjectives in **-ns**, add **-er** to the STEM:

Adjective	Stem	Adverb
dīligēns (*gen.* **dīligentis**)	**dīligent-**	**dīligenter**
careful		*carefully*

108   c. To form adverbs from many adjectives (especially of quantity and number), use the neuter singular accusative:

Adjective	Adverb
multus, a, um	multum
much	*much*
facilis, e	facile
easy	*easily*

Comparison of Adverbs.

109   a. The COMPARATIVE of an adverb is the same as the NEUTER ACCUSATIVE SINGULAR of the comparative adjective.

110   b. The SUPERLATIVE of the adverb is formed by changing the -us of the superlative adjective to -ē.

	Positive	*Comparative*	*Superlative*
Adj.	lātus, a, um	lātior, latius	lātissimus, a, um
	wide	*wider*	*widest*
Adv.	lātē	lātius	lātissimē
	widely	*more widely*	*most widely*
Adj.	facilis, e	facilior, facilius	facillimus, a, um
	easy	*easier*	*easiest*
Adv.	facile	facilius	facillimē
	easily	*more easily*	*most easily*

111   Irregular Comparison of Adverbs.

The following are irregular (either in the positive or in the comparative and superlative):

bene,[1] *well*	melius, *better*	optimē, *best*
male,[1] *badly*	pējus, *worse*	pessimē, *worst*
magnōpere,[2] *greatly*	magis, *more*	maximē, *most*
multum, *much*	plūs, *more*	plūrimum, *most*
parum, *(too) little*	minus, *less*	minimē, *least*
diū, *long* (of time)	diūtius, *longer*	diūtissimē, *longest*
nūper, *lately*	....	nūperrimē, *most recently*
....	potius, *rather*	potissimum, *especially*
prope, *near*	propius, *nearer*	proximē, *next*
saepe, *often*	saepius, *oftener*	saepissimē, *oftenest*

---

[1]Note the short final *e* in these adverbs.
[2]*Magnōpere = magnō opere* (from *opus, operis,* n.).

NUMERALS

Cardinals   Ordinals

	Cardinals	Ordinals
1	ūnus, a, um *(one)*	prīmus, a, um *(first)*
2	duo, ae, o *(two)*	secundus, a, um *(second)*[1]
3	trēs, tria	tertius, a, um
4	quattuor	quārtus, a, um
5	quīnque	quīntus, a, um
6	sex	sextus, a, um
7	septem	septimus, a, um
8	octō	octāvus, a, um
9	novem	nōnus, a, um
10	decem	decimus, a, um
11	ūndecim	ūndecimus, a, um
12	duodecim	duodecimus, a, um
13	tredecim	tertius (a, um) decimus, a, um
14	quattuordecim	quārtus (a, um) decimus, a, um
15	quīndecim	quīntus (a, um) decimus, a, um
16	sēdecim	sextus (a, um) decimus, a, um
17	septendecim	septimus (a, um) decimus, a, um
18	duodēvīgintī	duodēvīcēsimus, a, um
19	ūndēvīgintī	ūndēvīcēsimus, a, um
20	vīgintī	vīcēsimus, a, um
30	trīgintā	trīcēsimus, a, um
40	quadrāgintā	quadrāgēsimus, a, um
50	quīnquāgintā	quīnquāgēsimus, a, um
60	sexāgintā	sexāgēsimus, a, um
70	septuāgintā	septuāgēsimus, a, um
80	octōgintā	octōgēsimus, a, um
90	nōnāgintā	nōnāgēsimus, a, um
100	centum	centēsimus, a, um
200	ducentī, ae, a	ducentēsimus, a, um

---

[1]See No. 826.

28

300	trecentī, ae, a	trecentēsimus, a, um
400	quadringentī, ae, a	quadringentēsimus, a, um
500	quīngentī, ae, a	quīngentēsimus, a, um
600	sescentī, ae, a	sescentēsimus, a, um
700	septingentī, ae, a	septingentēsimus, a, um
800	octingentī, ae, a	octingentēsimus, a, um
900	nōngentī, ae, a	nōngentēsimus, a, um
1,000	mīlle	mīllēsimus, a, um
2,000	duo mīlia	bis[1] mīllēsimus, a, um
100,000	centum mīlia	centiēs[1] mīllēsimus, a, um
1,000,000	deciēs[1] centēna (ōrum) mīlia	deciēs centiēs mīllēsimus, a, um

Declension of Numerals.

114   a. **Ūnus, a, um,** *one,* is declined like **magnus, a, um** except in the genitive and dative singular.

	Masc.	*Fem.*	*Neut.*
Nom.	ūn-us	ūn-a	ūn-um
Gen.	ūn-īus	ūn-īus	ūn-īus
Dat.	ūn-ī	ūn-ī	ūn-ī
Acc.	ūn-um	ūn-am	ūn-um
Abl.	ūn-ō	ūn-ā	ūn-ō

115   b. **Duo, duae, duo,** *two.*

	Masc.	*Fem.*	*Neut.*
Nom.	duo	duae	duo
Gen.	duōrum	duārum	duōrum
Dat.	duōbus	duābus	duōbus
Acc.	duōs, duo	duās	duo
Abl.	duōbus	duābus	duōbus

---

[1]*Bis,* 'twice,' *deciēs,* 'ten times,' and *centiēs,* 'a hundred times,' are numerical adverbs (No. 118).

116   c. Trēs, tria, *three*, is declined like the plural of gravis, e.

	Masc.	*Fem.*	*Neut.*
Nom.	tr-ēs	tr-ēs	tr-ia
Gen.	tr-ium	tr-ium	tr-ium, *etc.*

117   d. Mīlle, *a thousand*, is an indeclinable ADJECTIVE:

> *a thousand men*, mīlle hominēs
>
> *by a thousand soldiers*, ā mīlle mīlitibus.

Mīlia, *thousands*, is a plural neuter NOUN (mīlia, mīlium, mīlibus, mīlia, mīlibus) and always takes the GENITIVE:

> *with three thousand soldiers*, cum tribus mīlibus mīlitum *(with three thousands of soldiers)*.
>
> *two thousand men*, duo mīlia hominum

All other declinable numerals are declined like the plural of magnus, a, um, thus: ducentī, ae, a, *two hundred*. Centum, *one hundred*, is indeclinable.

118   Note: In CARDINAL numbers the DISTRIBUTIVE centēnī and the numerical ADVERBS begin at 1,000,000 —deciēs centēna mīlia (literally, *ten times a hundred thousands*); in ORDINAL numbers the numerical ADVERBS begin at 2,000—bis mīllēsimus (literally, *two times a thousand*). The DISTRIBUTIVE numerals and the numerical ADVERBS are:

	Distributives	*Adverbs*
1	singulī, ae, a *(one by one)*	semel *(once)*
2	bīnī, ae, a *(two by two)*	bis *(twice)*
3	ternī (trīnī)	ter
4	quaternī	quater
10	dēnī	deciēs
20	vīcēnī	vīciēs
21	vīcēnī singulī	vīciēs semel
100	centēnī	centiēs

119 **Compound Numerals.**

The numerals 21-29, 31-39, *etc.*, are formed by using other numerals together:

120 a. For all the numerals compounded with 8 and 9 up to and inclusive of 88 and 89, prefix **duodē-** and **ūndē-** to the next zero number:

twenty-eight,	**duodētrīgintā**
	(two-from-thirty)
twenty-eighth,	**duodētrīcēsimus, a, um**
	(two-from-thirtieth)
thirty-nine,	**ūndēquadrāgintā**
	(one-from-forty)
thirty-ninth,	**ūndēquadrāgēsimus, a, um**
	(one-from-fortieth)

121 b. For all other compound numerals between 20 and 100 put the small number first and use **et,** or put the large number first without **et:**

twenty-one,	**ūnus et vīgintī**
	vīgintī ūnus
twenty-first,	**prīmus et vīcēsimus**
	vīcēsimus prīmus
ninety-four,	**quattuor et nōnāgintā**
	nōnāgintā quattuor
ninety-fourth,	**quārtus et nōnāgēsimus**
	nōnāgēsimus quārtus

122 c. From 101 up put the largest number first without **et:**

one hundred and one,	**centum ūnus**
one hundred and first,	**centēsimus prīmus**
one hundred and fifty-two,	**centum quīnquāgintā duo**

PRONOUNS

Personal Pronouns of the First and Second Persons.

123

First Person

	Nom.	ego	I	
	Gen.	meī	of me	of myself
S.	Dat.	mihi	to me	to myself
	Acc.	mē	me	myself
	Abl.	mē[1]	(by, etc.) me	(by, etc.) myself

	Nom.	nōs	we	
	Gen.	nostrī[2]	of us	of ourselves
P.		nostrum[3]		
	Dat.	nōbīs	to us	to ourselves
	Acc.	nōs	us	ourselves
	Abl.	nōbīs[1]	(by, etc.) us	(by, etc.) ourselves

124

Second Person

	Nom.	tū	you	
	Gen.	tuī	of you	of yourself
S.	Dat.	tibi	to you	to yourself
	Acc.	tē	you	yourself
	Abl.	tē[1]	(by, etc.) you	(by, etc.) yourself

	Nom.	vōs	you	
	Gen.	vestrī[2]	of you	of yourselves
P.		vestrum[3]		
	Dat.	vōbīs	to you	to yourselves
	Acc.	vōs	you	yourselves
	Abl.	vōbīs[1]	(by, etc.) you	(by, etc.) yourselves

---

[1]*Mēcum, tēcum, nōbīscum, vōbīscum* are used for *cum mē*, etc.
[2]*Nostrī* and *vestrī* are objective genitives only (see No. 684).
[3]*Nostrum* and *vestrum* are used as partitive genitives (see No. 686).

125 Possessive Adjectives and Pronouns of the First and Second Persons.[1]

	as adjective	as pronoun
meus, a, um	*my*	*mine*
noster, nostra, nostrum	*our*	*ours*
tuus, a, um	*your (singular)*	*yours*
vester, vestra, vestrum	*your (plural)*	*yours*

126 Meus, a, um and tuus, a, um are declined like magnus, a, um.

Noster, nostra, nostrum (stem: nostr-) and vester, vestra, vestrum (stem: vestr-) are declined like integer, integra, integrum.

---

[1]The possessive adjective is used more frequently than the personal pronoun. Thus *pater noster* is preferred to *pater nostrī*.

Personal Pronouns of the Third Person.

127   **a. Reflexive:**

Nom.	....	....
Gen.	suī	*of himself, herself, itself, themselves*
Dat.	sibi	*to himself, herself, itself, themselves*
Acc.	sē (sēsē)	*himself, herself, itself, themselves*
Abl.	sē[1] (sēsē)	*(by, etc.) himself, herself, itself, themselves*

128   **b. Non-reflexive:**

	Masc.		*Fem.*		*Neut.*	
Nom.	is	*he*	ea	*she*	id	*it*
Gen.	ējus	*of him his*	ējus	*of her her*	ējus	*of it its*
S. *Dat.*	eī	*to or for him*	eī	*to or for her*	eī	*to or for it*
Acc.	eum	*him*	eam	*her*	id	*it*
Abl.	eō	*(by, etc.) him*	eā	*(by, etc.) her*	eō	*(by, etc.) it*
Nom.	eī[2]	*they*	eae	*they*	ea	*they (those things)*
Gen.	eōrum	*of them their*	eārum	*of them their*	eōrum	*of them their*
P. *Dat.*	eīs[3]	*to or for them*	eīs[3]	*to or for them*	eīs[3]	*to or for them*
Acc.	eōs	*them*	eās	*them*	ea	*them (those things)*
Abl.	eīs[3]	*(by, etc.) them*	eīs[3]	*(by, etc.) them*	eīs[3]	*(by, etc.) them*

---

[1] *Sēcum* is used for *cum sē.*

[2] The nominative masculine plural is also spelled *ī.*

[3] The dative and ablative plural (all genders) are also spelled *īs.*

Note:

129   1. The meanings given for the masculine and feminine of **is, ea, id** hold only when the pronoun refers to PERSONS. Otherwise all forms are translated as in the neuter.

> Urbem cēpit. Posteā <u>eam</u> incendit.
> *He took the city. Afterwards he burned <u>it</u>.*

130   2. The plural is declined by adding the **plural** endings of **magnus, a, um** to the STEM, **e-.**

Possessive Adjective and Pronoun of the Third Person.

131   a. **Reflexive: suus, a, um,** *his (own), her (own), its (own), their (own).* **Suus** is declined like **magnus, a, um.**

132   b. **Non-reflexive:** The genitive of **is, ea, id** is used.

> **ējus,** *of him, of her, of it* = *his, her, its.*
> **eōrum, eārum,** *of them* = *their.*

Demonstrative Adjectives and Pronouns.

133

THIS

		Masc.	Fem.	Neut.
	Nom.	hic	haec	hoc
	Gen.	hūjus	hūjus	hūjus
S.	Dat.	huic	huic	huic
	Acc.	hunc	hanc	hoc
	Abl.	hōc	hāc	hōc

THESE

		Masc.	Fem.	Neut.
	Nom.	hī	hae	haec
	Gen.	hōrum	hārum	hōrum
P.	Dat.	hīs	hīs	hīs
	Acc.	hōs	hās	haec
	Abl.	hīs	hīs	hīs

134

THAT
(Emphatic)

		Masc.	Fem.	Neut.
	Nom.	ille	illa	illud
	Gen.	illīus	illīus	illīus
S.	Dat.	illī	illī	illī
	Acc.	illum	illam	illud
	Abl.	illō	illā	illō

THOSE

		Masc.	Fem.	Neut.
	Nom.	illī	illae	illa
	Gen.	illōrum	illārum	illōrum
P.	Dat.	illīs	illīs	illīs
	Acc.	illōs	illās	illa
	Abl.	illīs	illīs	illīs

135 Is, ea, id[1] is also a demonstrative pronoun meaning *that* (pl. *those*). It is less emphatic than ille, illa, illud.

136 Iste, ista, istud, *that, that of yours,* is declined like ille, illa, illud (No. 134).

137   SAME

		Masc.	*Fem.*	*Neut.*
	Nom.	īdem	eadem	idem
	Gen.	ējusdem	ējusdem	ējusdem
S.	Dat.	eīdem	eīdem	eīdem
	Acc.	eundem	eandem	idem
	Abl.	eōdem	eādem	eōdem
	Nom.	eīdem[2]	eaedem	eadem
	Gen.	eōrundem	eārundem	eōrundem
P.	Dat.	eīsdem[3]	eīsdem[3]	eīsdem[3]
	Acc.	eōsdem	eāsdem	eadem
	Abl.	eīsdem[3]	eīsdem[3]	eīsdem[3]

---

[1] This is the same word that is used for the personal pronoun of the third person. For its declension see No. 128.

[2] *Eīdem* is also spelled *īdem* and *īidem*.

[3] *Eīsdem* is also spelled *īsdem* and *īisdem*.

138   Intensive Adjective and Pronoun.

		Masc.	Fem.	Neut.
	Nom.	ipse	ipsa	ipsum
	Gen.	ipsīus	ipsīus	ipsīus
S.	Dat.	ipsī	ipsī	ipsī
	Acc.	ipsum	ipsam	ipsum
	Abl.	ipsō	ipsā	ipsō
	Nom.	ipsī	ipsae	ipsa
	Gen.	ipsōrum	ipsārum	ipsōrum
P.	Dat.	ipsīs	ipsīs	ipsīs
	Acc.	ipsōs	ipsās	ipsa
	Abl.	ipsīs	ipsīs	ipsīs

139   The Relative Pronoun and Adjective.

WHO; WHICH; THAT; WHAT

		Masc.	Fem.	Neut.
	Nom.	quī	quae	quod
	Gen.	cūjus	cūjus	cūjus
S.	Dat.	cui	cui	cui
	Acc.	quem	quam	quod
	Abl.	quō[1]	quā[1]	quō[1]
	Nom.	quī	quae	quae
	Gen.	quōrum	quārum	quōrum
P.	Dat.	quibus	quibus	quibus
	Acc.	quōs	quās	quae
	Abl.	quibus[1]	quibus[1]	quibus[1]

---

[1]*Quōcum* (or *quīcum*), *quācum*, *quibuscum* are used instead of *cum quŏ, cum quā, cum quibus.*

140 The Interrogative Pronoun.

WHO? WHAT?

		[*For Persons*]		*Neut.*
	Nom.	quis	quis	quid
	Gen.	cūjus	cūjus	cūjus
S.	*Dat.*	cui	cui	cui
	Acc.	quem	quem	quid
	Abl.	quō¹	quō¹	quō¹

		Masc.	*Fem.*	*Neut.*
	Nom.	quī	quae	quae
	Gen.	quōrum	quārum	quōrum
P.	*Dat.*	quibus	quibus	quibus
	Acc.	quōs	quās	quae
	Abl.	quibus¹	quibus¹	quibus¹

141 The Interrogative Adjective. Quī, quae, quod, *which, what,* is declined like the relative pronoun (No. 139).²

---

¹*Quōcum* (or *quīcum*) and *quibuscum* are used instead of *cum quō, cum quibus.*

²In the nominative masculine singular *quis* is generally used (especially with words denoting a person) as an adjective for 'which,' 'what' (*Quis vir vocat?* i. e., Give me the name of the man who is calling), and *quī* is used for the adjective 'what sort of,' 'what kind of' (*Quī homō ōrat?*).

VERBS

142   **Verbs** have voice, mood, tense, number, and person.

143   **Voice.** There are two voices: active and passive.

144   a. The active represents the subject as acting or being.

> Lēgātum laudō.
> *I praise the envoy.*
>
> Valeō.
> *I am well.*

145   b. The passive represents the subject as acted upon.

> Laudor.
> *I am praised.*

146   **Mood.**[1] There are three moods: indicative, subjunctive, imperative.

147   **Tense.**[1] There are six tenses: present, imperfect, future, perfect, pluperfect, future perfect.

148   **Number.** There are two numbers: singular and plural.

149   **Person.** There are three persons:
First (the one speaking—*I, we*).
Second (the one spoken to—*you*).
Third (the one spoken of—*he, she, it, they*).

150   **Conjugation** consists in adding the proper endings to the proper stem to show the different voices, moods, tenses, numbers, and persons.

---

[1]The meanings and uses of the moods and tenses must be learned from syntax.

151 The Four Conjugations. There are four conjugations in Latin. They can be distinguished by the endings of the present infinitive active.

	1	2	3	4
	-āre	-ēre	-ere	-īre
	laud-āre	mon-ēre	mitt-ere	aud-īre

152 Principal Parts. There are four parts of the verb called principal parts because all the others are formed on them or on their stems. These parts are:

	1	2	3	4
Pres. ind. act.	laud-ō	mon-eō	mitt-ō	aud-iō
Pres. infin. act.	laud-āre	mon-ēre	mitt-ere	aud-īre
Perf. ind. act.	laudāv-ī	monu-ī	mīs-ī	audīv-ī
Perf. part. pass.	laudāt-us[1]	monit-us[1]	miss-us[1]	audīt-us[1]

153 The **present stem** is found by dropping the ending of the present infinitive active.

laudāre	laud-	On this stem are formed: all present, imperfect, and future tenses;[2] the gerund and the gerundive.
monēre	mon-	
mittere	mitt-	
audīre	aud-	

154 The **perfect stem** is found by dropping the ending of the perfect indicative.

laudāvī	laudāv-	On this stem are formed: all perfect, pluperfect, future perfect tenses active.
monuī	monu-	
mīsī	mīs-	
audīvī	audīv-	

---

[1]The perfect participle passive is given in the masculine in all verbs that use it in all genders; otherwise it is given in the neuter (*e. g.*, in intransitive verbs). Some verbs have no perfect participle passive; the future participle active is then given as the fourth principal part (*e. g.*, *haereō, haerēre, haesī, haesūrus, 2, intr.*, 'cling').

[2]Except the future participle active and the future infinitive passive (see Nos. 156 and 158).

155   The **perfect participle passive** is used with forms of the
verb **esse** to form the perfect, pluperfect, future perfect
tenses passive.

laudātus	laudātus sum, *etc.*
monitus	monitus sum, *etc.*
missus	missus sum, *etc.*
audītus	audītus sum, *etc.*

Other Uses of the Perfect Participle Passive:

156   1. The **future participle active** is formed by changing the
-us of the perfect participle passive to -ūrus.

157   2. The **supines** are formed by changing the -us of the perfect participle passive to -um or to -ū.

158   3. The **future infinitive passive** is formed on this stem
by using the supine in -um with īrī as a separate word.

Perf. Part. Pass.	*Fut. Part. Act.*	*Supines*		*Fut. Inf. Pass.*
laudātus	laudāt-ūrus	laudāt-um	laudāt-ū	laudātum īrī
monitus	monit-ūrus	monit-um	monit-ū	monitum īrī
missus	miss-ūrus	miss-um	miss-ū	missum īrī
audītus	audīt-ūrus	audīt-um	audīt-ū	audītum īrī

159   How to Conjugate.

1. The principal parts must be learned from the vocabularies.[1]
2. The present infinitive shows to which conjugation the
verb belongs.
3. Find the required stems according to the rules given
above.
4. Add the endings of the proper conjugation to the stems.

---

[1]But many verbs of the first, second, and fourth conjugations form their
principal parts just like *laudō, moneō, audiō.* These will be written in
the vocabularies: *pācō, 1, tr.,* 'pacify,' *etc.* The principal parts of verbs
of the third conjugation, however, will always be written out.

THE FOUR REGULAR CONJUGATIONS

Model Verbs

Laudō, laudāre, laudāvī, laudātus, *1, tr., praise*

Moneō, monēre, monuī, monitus, *2, tr., advise*

Mittō, mittere, mīsī, missus, *3, tr., send*

Audiō, audīre, audīvī, audītus, *4, tr., hear*

ACTIVE VOICE

160   **Personal Signs of the Active.**

		Singular		*Plural*
First	*(I)*	-ō or -m	*(we)*	-mus
Second	*(you)*	-s	*(you)*	-tis
Third	*(he, she, it)*	-t	*(they)*	-nt

161   **Exceptions:** First and second person singular perfect indicative: **laudāv-ī** and **laudāv-istī.**

ACTIVE VOICE
INDICATIVE MOOD

Present Tense
(Present Stem)

162

S.	1.	laud-ō	*I praise, I am praising, I do praise*
	2.	laud-ās	*you praise, you are praising, you do praise*
	3.	laud-at	*he, she, it praises; he, she, it is praising; he, she, it does praise*

P.	1.	laud-āmus	*we praise, we are praising, we do praise*
	2.	laud-ātis	*you praise, you are praising, you do praise*
	3.	laud-ant	*they praise, they are praising, they do praise*

Imperfect Tense
(Present Stem)

163

S.	1.	laud-ābam	*I was praising*
	2.	laud-ābās	*you were praising*
	3.	laud-ābat	*he, she, it was praising*

P.	1.	laud-ābāmus	*we were praising*
	2.	laud-ābātis	*you were praising*
	3.	laud-ābant	*they were praising*

Future Tense
(Present Stem)

164

S.	1.	laud-ābō	*I shall praise*	*(I shall be praising)*
	2.	laud-ābis	*you will praise*	*(you will be praising)*
	3.	laud-ābit	*he, she, it will praise*	*(he, she, it will be praising)*

P.	1.	laud-ābimus	*we shall praise*	*(we shall be praising)*
	2.	laud-ābitis	*you will praise*	*(you will be praising)*
	3.	laud-ābunt	*they will praise*	*(they will be praising)*

ACTIVE VOICE
INDICATIVE MOOD

Present Tense
(Present Stem)

	I advise,		*I send,*		*I hear.*
165	mon-eō	**166**	mitt-ō	**167**	aud-iō
	mon-ēs		mitt-is		aud-īs
	mon-et		mitt-it		aud-it
	mon-ēmus		mitt-imus		aud-īmus
	mon-ētis		mitt-itis		aud-ītis
	mon-ent		mitt-unt		aud-iunt

Imperfect Tense
(Present Stem)

	I was advising,		*sending,*		*hearing.*
168	mon-ēbam	**169**	mitt-ēbam	**170**	aud-iēbam
	mon-ēbās		mitt-ēbās		aud-iēbās
	mon-ēbat		mitt-ēbat		aud-iēbat
	mon-ēbāmus		mitt-ēbāmus		aud-iēbāmus
	mon-ēbātis		mitt-ēbātis		aud-iēbātis
	mon-ēbant		mitt-ēbant		aud-iēbant

Future Tense
(Present Stem)

	I shall advise,		*send,*		*hear.*
171	mon-ēbō	**172**	mitt-am	**173**	aud-iam
	mon-ēbis		mitt-ēs		aud-iēs
	mon-ēbit		mitt-et		aud-iet
	mon-ēbimus		mitt-ēmus		aud-iēmus
	mon-ēbitis		mitt-ētis		aud-iētis
	mon-ēbunt		mitt-ent		aud-ient

ACTIVE VOICE

INDICATIVE MOOD

Perfect Tense
(Perfect Stem)

174

S.
1. laudāv-ī   *I praised*   *(I have praised)*
2. laudāv-istī   *you praised*   *(you have praised)*
3. laudāv-it   *he, she, it praised*   *(he, she, it has praised)*

P.
1. laudāv-imus   *we praised*   *(we have praised)*
2. laudāv-istis   *you praised*   *(you have praised)*
3. laudāv-ērunt   *they praised*   *(they have praised)*

Pluperfect Tense
*(Perfect Stem and the Imperfect of **sum**)*

175

S.
1. laudāv-eram   *I had praised*
2. laudāv-erās   *you had praised*
3. laudāv-erat   *he, she, it had praised*

P.
1. laudāv-erāmus   *we had praised*
2. laudāv-erātis   *you had praised*
3. laudāv-erant   *they had praised*

Future Perfect Tense
(Perfect Stem)

176

S.
1. laudāv-erō   *I shall have praised*
2. laudāv-eris   *you will have praised*
3. laudāv-erit   *he, she, it will have praised*

P.
1. laudāv-erimus   *we shall have praised*
2. laudāv-eritis   *you will have praised*
3. laudāv-erint   *they will have praised*

ACTIVE VOICE

INDICATIVE MOOD

Perfect Tense
(Perfect Stem)

I (have) advised,	*sent,*	*heard.*
177 monu-ī	**178** mīs-ī	**179** audīv-ī
monu-istī	mīs-istī	audīv-istī
monu-it	mīs-it	audīv-it
monu-imus	mīs-imus	audīv-imus
monu-istis	mīs-istis	audīv-istis
monu-ērunt	mīs-ērunt	audīv-ērunt

Pluperfect Tense
*(Perfect Stem and the Imperfect of **sum**)*

I had advised,	*sent,*	*heard.*
180 monu-eram	**181** mīs-eram	**182** audīv-eram
monu-erās	mīs-erās	audīv-erās
monu-erat	mīs-erat	audīv-erat
monu-erāmus	mīs-erāmus	audīv-erāmus
monu-erātis	mīs-erātis	audīv-erātis
monu-erant	mīs-erant	audīv-erant

Future Perfect Tense
(Perfect Stem)

I shall have advised,	*sent,*	*heard.*
183 monu-erō	**184** mīs-erō	**185** audīv-erō
monu-eris	mīs-eris	audīv-eris
monu-erit	mīs-erit	audīv-erit
monu-erimus	mīs-erimus	audīv-erimus
monu-eritis	mīs-eritis	audīv-eritis
monu-erint	mīs-erint	audīv-erint

ACTIVE VOICE

SUBJUNCTIVE MOOD

Present Tense
(Present Stem)

			In Purpose Clauses	In Wishes
186		1. laud-em	*(that) I may praise*	*may I praise*
	S.	2. laud-ēs	*(that) you may praise*	*may you praise*
		3. laud-et	*(that) he, she, it may praise*	*may he, she, it praise*
		1. laud-ēmus	*(that) we may praise*	*may we praise,*
	P.	2. laud-ētis	*(that) you may praise*	*may you praise*
		3. laud-ent	*(that) they may praise*	*may they praise*

Imperfect Tense
(Present Stem)

187		1. laud-ārem	*(that) I might praise*
	S.	2. laud-ārēs	*(that) you might praise*
		3. laud-āret	*(that) he, she, it might praise*
		1. laud-ārēmus	*(that) we might praise*
	P.	2. laud-ārētis	*(that) you might praise*
		3. laud-ārent	*(that) they might praise*

Examples of the Subjunctive

188 The meanings of the subjunctive must be learned from syntax. A few examples are given here.

189 1. The present subjunctive is used to express wishes, as:

> *May you praise God.*
> Deum <u>laudēs.</u>

190 2. The first person plural and the third person, singular and plural, of the present subjunctive are used to translate the English *let*, as:

> <u>*Let us praise* God.</u>
> Deum laudēmus.

ACTIVE VOICE

SUBJUNCTIVE MOOD

Present Tense
(Present Stem)

	(that) I may advise,		send,		hear.
194	mon-eam	**195**	mitt-am	**196**	aud-iam
	mon-eās		mitt-ās		aud-iās
	mon-eat		mitt-at		aud-iat
	mon-eāmus		mitt-āmus		aud-iāmus
	mon-eātis		mitt-ātis		aud-iātis
	mon-eant		mitt-ant		aud-iant

Imperfect Tense
(Present Stem)

	(that) I might advise,		send,		hear.
197	mon-ērem	**198**	mitt-erem	**199**	aud-īrem
	mon-ērēs		mitt-erēs		aud-īrēs
	mon-ēret		mitt-eret		aud-īret
	mon-ērēmus		mitt-erēmus		aud-īrēmus
	mon-ērētis		mitt-erētis		aud-īrētis
	mon-ērent		mitt-erent		aud-īrent

191   3. The present and imperfect subjunctive are used in subordinate purpose clauses:

$$Christ\ came\ \begin{cases} \underline{that\ He\ might} \\ \underline{to} \end{cases} \underline{praise}\ God.$$

Chrīstus vēnit ut Deum <u>laudāret.</u>

192   4. The subjunctive is used in indirect questions.

He asked whether I was praising God.
Rogāvit num Deum laudārem.

193   **Note:** The subjunctive in subordinate clauses is often translated by the ENGLISH INDICATIVE.

ACTIVE VOICE

SUBJUNCTIVE MOOD

Perfect Tense
(Perfect Active Stem)

In Indirect Questions

200

	1.	**laudāv-erim**	*(whether) I praised*
S.	2.	**laudāv-erīs**	*(whether) you praised*
	3.	**laudāv-erit**	*(whether) he, she, it praised*
	1.	**laudāv-erīmus**	*(whether) we praised*
P.	2.	**laudāv-erītis**	*(whether) you praised*
	3.	**laudāv-erint**	*(whether) they praised*

Pluperfect Tense
(Perfect Active Stem)

201

	1.	**laudāv-issem**	*(whether) I had praised*
S.	2.	**laudāv-issēs**	*(whether) you had praised*
	3.	**laudāv-isset**	*(whether) he, she, it had praised*
	1.	**laudāv-issēmus**	*(whether) we had praised*
P.	2.	**laudāv-issētis**	*(whether) you had praised*
	3.	**laudāv-issent**	*(whether) they had praised*

ACTIVE VOICE

SUBJUNCTIVE MOOD

Perfect Tense
(Perfect Active Stem)

	(whether) I advised,		*sent,*		*heard.*
202	monu-erim	**203**	mīs-erim	**204**	audīv-erim
	monu-erīs		mīs-erīs		audīv-erīs
	monu-erit		mīs-erit		audīv-erit
	monu-erīmus		mīs-erīmus		audīv-erīmus
	monu-erītis		mīs-erītis		audīv-erītis
	monu-erint		mīs-erint		audīv-erint

Pluperfect Tense
(Perfect Active Stem)

	(whether) I had advised,		*sent,*		*heard.*
205	monu-issem	**206**	mīs-issem	**207**	audīv-issem
	monu-issēs		mīs-issēs		audīv-issēs
	monu-isset		mīs-isset		audīv-isset
	monu-issēmus		mīs-issēmus		audīv-issēmus
	monu-issētis		mīs-issētis		audīv-issētis
	monu-issent		mīs-issent		audīv-issent

ACTIVE VOICE

IMPERATIVE MOOD
(Present Stem)

208   *S.*   **laud-ā**   *(you) praise!*
       P.   **laud-āte**   *(you) praise!*

INFINITIVE

Present Tense *(Present Stem)*	Perfect Tense *(Perfect Active Stem)*
209 **laudāre** *to praise*	**210** **laudāv-isse** *to have praised*

Future Tense
(Stem of perfect participle passive, e. g., **laudātus***, stem:* **laudāt-***)*

211   **laudāt-ūrus, a, um esse**   *to be about to praise*

GERUND (VERBAL NOUN)
(Present Stem)

212
Gen.	**laud-andī**	*of praising*
Dat.	**laud-andō**	*to or for praising*
Acc.	**laud-andum**	*praising*
Abl.	**laud-andō**	*by praising*

SUPINE
(Stem of perfect participle passive, e. g., **laudātus***, stem:* **laudāt-***)*

213   **laudāt-um**   *to praise*
         laudāt-ū   *in praising, to praise*

PARTICIPLE (VERBAL ADJECTIVE)

Present Tense
(Present Stem)

214   **laudāns (laudant-is)**[1]   *praising*

Future Tense
(Stem of perfect participle passive, e. g., **laudātus***, stem:* **laudāt-***)*

215   **laudāt-ūrus, a, um**[2]
$\begin{cases} \textit{being about to praise} \\ \textit{about to praise} \\ \textit{on the point of praising} \end{cases}$

---

[1]For the declension of the present participle see No. 307.
[2]The future participle is declined like *magnus, a, um.*

ACTIVE VOICE

IMPERATIVE MOOD[1]
(Present Stem)

216 S. mon-ē   **217** mitt-e   **218** aud-ī
   P. mon-ēte   mitt-ite   aud-īte

INFINITIVE
Present Tense
(Present Stem)

219 mon-ēre   **220** mitt-ere   **221** aud-īre

Perfect Tense
(Perfect Active Stem)

222 monu-isse   **223** mīs-isse   **224** audīv-isse

Future Tense
(Stem of perfect participle passive, e. g., monitus, stem: monit-)

225 monit-ūrus, a, um esse   **226** miss-ūrus, a, um esse   **227** audīt-ūrus, a, um esse

GERUND (VERBAL NOUN)
(Present Stem)

228 Gen. mon-endī   **229** mitt-endī   **230** aud-iendī
   Dat. mon-endō   mitt-endō   aud-iendō
   Acc. mon-endum   mitt-endum   aud-iendum
   Abl. mon-endō   mitt-endō   aud-iendō

SUPINE
(Stem of perfect participle passive, e. g., monitus, stem: monit-)

231 monit-um   **232** miss-um   **233** audīt-um
   monit-ū   miss-ū   audīt-ū

---

[1]In the future the imperative occurs in both the second and third persons: singular, *laudātō (monētō, mittitō, audītō)*, 'you shall praise (advise, send, hear)'; *laudātō (monētō, mittitō, audītō)*, 'he shall praise (advise, send, hear)'; plural, *laudātōte (monētōte, mittitōte, audītōte)*, 'you shall praise (advise, send, hear)'; *laudantō (monentō, mittuntō, audiuntō)*, 'they shall praise (advise, send, hear).'

PARTICIPLE (VERBAL ADJECTIVE)

Present Tense
(Present Stem)

234	mon-ēns (monent-is)[1]	235	mitt-ēns (mittent-is)[1]	236	aud-iēns (audient-is)[1]

Future Tense
(Stem of perfect participle passive, e. g., monitus, *stem:* monit-*)*

237	monit-ūrus, a, um[2]	238	miss-ūrus, a, um[2]	239	audīt-ūrus, a, um[2]

---

[1]For the declension of the present participle see No. 307.
[2]The future participle is declined like *magnus, a, um.*

PASSIVE VOICE

To form the PASSIVE of the four regular conjugations:

240 a. In the finite tenses formed on the PRESENT STEM change the final personal signs:

Singular

1. -ō	to	-or
-m	to	-r
2. -s	to	-ris
3. -t	to	-tur

Plural

1. -mus	to	-mur
2. -tis	to	-minī
3. -nt	to	-ntur

241 Note: The second person singular of the future indicative in the first and second conjugations changes

-is to -eris

laudābis laudāberis
monēbis monēberis

242 b. In the perfect tenses use the perfect participle passive with the forms of the verb **esse** shown in Nos. 255-257, 275-276. Thus:

laudātus sum *I have been praised*
laudātus erās *you had been praised*

PASSIVE VOICE

INDICATIVE MOOD

Present Tense
(Present Stem)

243

S.
1.	laud-or	*I am being praised*	*(I am praised)*
2.	laud-āris	*you are being praised*	*(you are praised)*
3.	laud-ātur	*he, she, it is being praised*	*(he, she, it is praised)*

P.
1.	laud-āmur	*we are being praised*	*(we are praised)*
2.	laud-āminī	*you are being praised*	*(you are praised)*
3.	laud-antur	*they are being praised*	*(they are praised)*

Imperfect Tense
(Present Stem)

244

S.
1.	laud-ābar	*I was being praised*
2.	laud-ābāris	*you were being praised*
3.	laud-ābātur	*he, she, it was being praised*

P.
1.	laud-ābāmur	*we were being praised*
2.	laud-ābāminī	*you were being praised*
3.	laud-ābantur	*they were being praised*

Future Tense
(Present Stem)

245

S.
1.	laud-ābor	*I shall be praised*
2.	laud-āberis	*you will be praised*
3.	laud-ābitur	*he, she, it will be praised*

P.
1.	laud-ābimur	*we shall be praised*
2.	laud-ābiminī	*you will be praised*
3.	laud-ābuntur	*they will be praised*

PASSIVE VOICE

INDICATIVE MOOD

Present Tense
(Present Stem)

	I am advised,		*sent,*		*heard.*
246	mon-eor	**247**	mitt-or	**248**	aud-ior
	mon-ēris		mitt-eris		aud-īris
	mon-ētur		mitt-itur		aud-ītur
	mon-ēmur		mitt-imur		aud-īmur
	mon-ēminī		mitt-iminī		aud-īminī
	mon-entur		mitt-untur		aud-iuntur

Imperfect Tense
(Present Stem)

	I was being advised,		*sent,*		*heard.*
249	mon-ēbar	**250**	mitt-ēbar	**251**	aud-iēbar
	mon-ēbāris		mitt-ēbāris		aud-iēbāris
	mon-ēbātur		mitt-ēbātur		aud-iēbātur
	mon-ēbāmur		mitt-ēbāmur		aud-iēbāmur
	mon-ēbāminī		mitt-ēbāminī		aud-iēbāminī
	mon-ēbantur		mitt-ēbantur		aud-iēbantur

Future Tense
(Present Stem)

	I shall be advised,		*sent,*		*heard.*
252	mon-ēbor	**253**	mitt-ar	**254**	aud-iar
	mon-ēberis		mitt-ēris		aud-iēris
	mon-ēbitur		mitt-ētur		aud-iētur
	mon-ēbimur		mitt-ēmur		aud-iēmur
	mon-ēbiminī		mitt-ēminī		aud-iēminī
	mon-ēbuntur		mitt-entur		aud-ientur

PASSIVE VOICE

INDICATIVE MOOD

Perfect Tense

(Perfect participle passive with **sum,** *etc.)*

255   S. laudātus (a, um)

sum	*I was praised*	*(I have been praised)*
es	*you were praised*	*(you have been praised)*
est	*he, she, it was praised*	*(he, she, it has been praised)*

P. laudātī (ae, a)

sumus	*we were praised*	*(we have been praised)*
estis	*you were praised*	*(you have been praised)*
sunt	*they were praised*	*(they have been praised)*

Pluperfect Tense

(Perfect participle passive with **eram,** *etc.)*

256   S. laudātus (a, um)

eram	*I had been praised*
erās	*you had been praised*
erat	*he, she, it had been praised*

P. laudātī (ae, a)

erāmus	*we had been praised*
erātis	*you had been praised*
erant	*they had been praised*

Future Perfect Tense

(Perfect participle passive with **erō,** *etc.)*

257   S. laudātus (a, um)

erō	*I shall have been praised*
eris	*you will have been praised*
erit	*he, she, it will have been praised*

P. laudātī (ae, a)

erimus	*we shall have been praised*
eritis	*you will have been praised*
erunt	*they will have been praised*

PASSIVE VOICE

INDICATIVE MOOD

Perfect Tense
(Perfect participle passive with **sum,** *etc.)*

I was (have been) advised, sent,   heard.

258		259	260	
				⎧ sum
S.	monitus, a, um	missus, a, um	audītus, a, um	⎨ es
				⎩ est
				⎧ sumus
P.	monitī, ae, a	missī, ae, a	audītī, ae, a	⎨ estis
				⎩ sunt

Pluperfect Tense
(Perfect participle passive with **eram,** *etc.)*
I had been advised, sent,   heard.

261		262	263	
				⎧ eram
S.	monitus, a, um	missus, a, um	audītus, a, um	⎨ erās
				⎩ erat
				⎧ erāmus
P.	monitī, ae, a	missī, ae, a	audītī, ae, a	⎨ erātis
				⎩ erant

Future Perfect Tense
(Perfect participle passive with **erō,** *etc.)*

I shall have been advised, sent,   heard.

264		265	266	
				⎧ erō
S.	monitus, a, um	missus, a, um	audītus, a, um	⎨ eris
				⎩ erit
				⎧ erimus
P.	monitī, ae, a	missī, ae, a	audītī, ae, a	⎨ eritis
				⎩ erunt

PASSIVE VOICE

SUBJUNCTIVE MOOD

Present Tense
(Present Stem)

267

		In Purpose Clauses[1]	In Wishes
S.	1. **laud-er**	*(that) I may be praised*	*may I be praised*
	2. **laud-ēris**	*(that) you may be praised*	*may you be praised*
	3. **laud-ētur**	*(that) he, she, it may be praised*	*may he, she, it be praised*
P.	1. **laud-ēmur**	*(that) we may be praised*	*may we be praised*
	2. **laud-ēminī**	*(that) you may be praised*	*may you be praised*
	3. **laud-entur**	*(that) they may be praised*	*may they be praised*

Imperfect Tense
(Present Stem)

268

		In Purpose Clauses[1]
S.	1. **laud-ārer**	*(that) I might be praised*
	2. **laud-ārēris**	*(that) you might be praised*
	3. **laud-ārētur**	*(that) he, she, it might be praised*
P.	1. **laud-ārēmur**	*(that) we might be praised*
	2. **laud-ārēminī**	*(that) you might be praised*
	3. **laud-ārentur**	*(that) they might be praised*

---

[1]Example meanings of the subjunctive are given here. For other meanings see Nos. 189-193. Further treatment of the subjunctive will be found in Part 2, Syntax.

PASSIVE VOICE

SUBJUNCTIVE MOOD

Present Tense
(Present Stem)

	(that) I may be advised,		*sent,*		*heard.*
269	mon-ear	**270**	mitt-ar	**271**	aud-iar
	mon-eāris		mitt-āris		aud-iāris
	mon-eātur		mitt-ātur		aud-iātur
	mon-eāmur		mitt-āmur		aud-iāmur
	mon-eāminī		mitt-āminī		aud-iāminī
	mon-eantur		mitt-antur		aud-iantur

Imperfect Tense
(Present Stem)

	(that) I might be advised,		*sent,*		*heard.*
272	mon-ērer	**273**	mitt-erer	**274**	aud-īrer
	mon-ērēris		mitt-erēris		aud-īrēris
	mon-ērētur		mitt-erētur		aud-īrētur
	mon-ērēmur		mitt-erēmur		aud-īrēmur
	mon-ērēminī		mitt-erēminī		aud-īrēminī
	mon-ērentur		mitt-erentur		aud-īrentur

PASSIVE VOICE

SUBJUNCTIVE MOOD

Perfect Tense
(*Perfect participle passive* with **sim,** *etc.*)

In Indirect Questions

275   S.   **laudātus, a, um**

	sim	*(whether) I was praised*	*(I have been praised)*
	sīs	*(whether) you were praised*	*(you have been praised)*
	sit	*(whether) he, she, it was praised*	*(he, she, it has been praised)*

     P.   **laudātī, ae, a**

	sīmus	*(whether) we were praised*	*(we have been praised)*
	sītis	*(whether) you were praised*	*(you have been praised)*
	sint	*(whether) they were praised*	*(they have been praised)*

Pluperfect Tense
(*Perfect participle passive* with **essem,** *etc.*)

In Indirect Questions

276   S.   **laudātus, a, um**

	essem	*(whether) I had been praised*
	essēs	*(whether) you had been praised*
	esset	*(whether) he, she, it had been praised*

     P.   **laudātī, ae, a**

	essēmus	*(whether) we had been praised*
	essētis	*(whether) you had been praised*
	essent	*(whether) they had been praised*

PASSIVE VOICE

SUBJUNCTIVE MOOD

Perfect Tense
(Perfect participle passive with **sim**, *etc.)*

(whether) I was advised, sent,   heard.

277	278	279	
S. monitus, a, um	missus, a, um	audītus, a, um	sim sīs sit
P. monitī, ae, a	missī, ae, a	audītī, ae, a	sīmus sītis sint

Pluperfect Tense
(Perfect participle passive with **essem**, *etc.)*

(whether) I had been advised, sent,   heard.

280	281	282	
S. monitus, a, um	missus, a, um	audītus, a, um	essem essēs esset
P. monitī, ae, a	missī, ae, a	audītī, ae, a	essēmus essētis essent

PASSIVE VOICE

IMPERATIVE MOOD[1]
(Present Stem)

283　S.　laud-āre　　　　*be (you) praised!*
　　　P.　laud-āminī　　　*be (you) praised!*

INFINITIVE

Present Tense
(Present Stem)

284　laud-ārī　　　　　　*to be praised*

Perfect Tense
(Perfect participle passive with **esse***)*

285　laudātus, a, um esse　*to have been praised*

Future Tense
(Supine with **īrī***)*

286　laudāt-um īrī　　　　*to be about to be praised*

PARTICIPLE (VERBAL ADJECTIVE)
Perfect Tense

287　laudāt-us, a, um[2]　　*having been praised*

GERUNDIVE
(Present Stem)

288　laud-andus, a, um[2]　　*(ought) to be praised*

---

[1] In the future the imperative occurs in both the second and third persons singular and the third person plural: singular, *laudātor,* 'you shall be praised,' *laudātor,* 'he shall be praised'; plural, *laudantor,* 'they shall be praised.' The second person plural may be supplied by the future indicative passive: *laudābiminī.*

[2] Declined like *magnus, a, um.*

PASSIVE VOICE

IMPERATIVE MOOD[1]
(Present Stem)

289 mon-ēre	290 mitt-ere	291 aud-īre
mon-ēminī	mitt-iminī	aud-īminī

INFINITIVE

Present Tense
(Present Stem)

292 mon-ērī	293 mitt-ī	294 aud-īrī

Perfect Tense
(Perfect participle passive with **esse**)

295 monitus, a, um	296 missus, a, um	297 audītus, a, um
esse	esse	esse

Future Tense
(Supine with **īrī**)

298 monit-um īrī	299 miss-um īrī	300 audīt-um īrī

PARTICIPLE (VERBAL ADJECTIVE)
Perfect Tense

301 monit-us, a, um[2]	302 miss-us, a, um[2]	303 audīt-us, a, um[2]

GERUNDIVE
(Present Stem)

304	305	306
mon-endus, a, um[2]	mitt-endus, a, um[2]	aud-iendus, a, um[2]

---

[1]The forms of the future imperative are: *monētor (mittitor, audītor)*, 'you shall be advised (sent, heard)'; *monētor, (mittitor, audītor)*, 'he shall be advised (sent, heard)'; *monentor (mittuntor, audiuntor)*, 'they shall be advised (sent, heard).' The second person plural may be supplied by the future indicative passive: *monēbiminī, mittēminī, audiēminī*.

[2]Declined like *magnus, a, um*.

Declension of Participles.

307   a. The PRESENT PARTICIPLE ACTIVE is declined like dīligēns (dīligentis), No. 82, except in the ABLATIVE SINGULAR where it has **e.**

Thus:	laudāns	laudāns	laudāns
	laudant-is	laudant-is	laudant-is
	etc.	*etc.*	*etc.*
Abl.	laudante	laudante	laudante

Gallī fortiter <u>pugnantēs</u> occīsī sunt.

The Gauls <u>fighting</u> bravely were killed.

Deō <u>adjuvante,</u> vincēmus.

God <u>helping,</u> we shall conquer.

Note:

308   1. Occasionally a participle is used AS A NOUN.

     Ā <u>sapiente</u> doctus est.

     He was taught by a <u>wise man.</u>

309   2. A few participles may be used AS ADJECTIVES. The ablative then ends in **ī.**

     Caesar annō <u>īnsequentī</u> advēnit.

     Caesar arrived the <u>following</u> year.

310   b. ALL OTHER PARTICIPLES are declined like **magnus, a, um.**

     The future active: **laudātūrus, a, um**
       Stem: **laudātūr-**

     The perfect participle passive: **laudātus, a, um**
       Stem: **laudāt-**

     The gerundive: **laudandus, a, um**
       Stem: **laudand-**

-Iō Verbs of the Third Conjugation.

311 -Iō verbs of the third conjugation can be distinguished by the endings of the first and second principal parts (-iō and -ere). Thus: **capiō, capere, cēpī, captus,** *3, tr., take, capture.* These verbs have the endings of the FOURTH CONJUGATION in those forms where the endings of the fourth conjugation begin with TWO VOWELS: *e. g.,* **capiēbam.** In all other forms they have the endings of the THIRD CONJUGATION. In the conjugation of the model verb (pages 68-69) all forms using the endings of the third conjugation are printed in ITALICS.

CAPIŌ, CAPERE, CĒPĪ, CAPTUS, *3, tr., take, capture.*

ACTIVE VOICE

	INDICATIVE		SUBJUNCTIVE
	Present		*Present*

312 S. { capiō
    capis
    capit

315 capiam
    capiās
    capiat

P. { *capimus*
    capitis
    capiunt

    capiāmus
    capiātis
    capiant

    Imperfect   *Imperfect*

313 S. { capiēbam
    capiēbās
    capiēbat

316 *caperem*
    caperēs
    caperet

P. { capiēbāmus
    capiēbātis
    capiēbant

    caperēmus
    caperētis
    caperent

    Future

314 S. { capiam
    capiēs
    capiet

P. { capiēmus
    capiētis
    capient

IMPERATIVE

317 *S. cape*
    P. capite

INFINITIVE

318 *Pres. capere*

GERUND

319 *Gen.* capiendī
    Dat. capiendō
    Acc. capiendum
    Abl. capiendō

PARTICIPLE

320 *Pres.* capiēns
    (capient-is)

321 Note: All the tenses of the perfect system active are formed regularly on the perfect stem.

Thus: **cēp-ī, cēp-istī,** *etc.*

PASSIVE VOICE

INDICATIVE	SUBJUNCTIVE	IMPERATIVE

INDICATIVE

Present

322

S.
- capior
- caperis
- capitur

P.
- capimur
- capiminī
- capiuntur

Imperfect

323

S.
- capiēbar
- capiēbāris
- capiēbātur

P.
- capiēbāmur
- capiēbāminī
- capiēbantur

Future

324

S.
- capiar
- capiēris
- capiētur

P.
- capiēmur
- capiēminī
- capientur

SUBJUNCTIVE

Present

325
- capiar
- capiāris
- capiātur

- capiāmur
- capiāminī
- capiantur

Imperfect

326 *caperer*
- *capereris*
- *caperētur*

- *caperēmur*
- *caperēminī*
- *caperentur*

IMPERATIVE

327 S. *capere*
P. *capiminī*

INFINITIVE

328 *Pres.* capī

GERUNDIVE

329 capiendus,
a, um

330 Note: All the tenses of the perfect system passive are formed regularly by using the perfect participle passive with the required forms of **sum**.

Thus: **captus, a, um sum,
es,** *etc.*

Impersonal Verbs.

331   Impersonal verbs have no definite person or thing as their subject. They are used only in the THIRD PERSON SINGULAR of the indicative and subjunctive, and in the INFINITIVE. Whenever the tense is compound, the participle is NEUTER. In English the indefinite *it* serves as subject.

> Licet.
> *It is allowed.*

> Factum est.
> *It happened.*

> Pluit.
> *It rains.*

> Licēre dīcō.
> *I say (that) it is allowed.*

Note:

332   1. Many personal verbs are sometimes used impersonally, especially in the passive.

> Pugnō *(personal).*
> *I fight.*

> Ācriter pugnātum est *(impersonal).*
> *There was bitter fighting.*
> *(It was bitterly fought.)*

333   2. Many verbs, however, are used impersonally only. Their principal parts are given thus:

> **Licet, licēre, licuit, *2, intr.; dat. of person and infin., it is allowed.***

> Mihi venīre licet.
> *It is allowed (to) me to come.*

Deponent Verbs.

334 Some verbs have PASSIVE FORMS but ACTIVE MEAN-
INGS. These are called deponent verbs. They have only
three principal parts:

	1st Sing. *Pres. Indic.*	*Present* *Infin.*	*1st Sing. Perf.* *Indic.*
I	hortor	hortārī	hortātus sum, *1, tr.,* *exhort*
II	vereor	verērī	veritus sum, *2, tr.,* *fear*
III	sequor	sequī	secūtus sum, *3, tr.,* *follow*
III (-iō)	patior	patī	passus sum, *3, tr.,* *suffer*
IV	mōlior	mōlīrī	mōlītus sum, *4, tr.,* *set in motion*

335 Deponents are conjugated exactly like **laudor, moneor,
mittor, capior, audior** (Nos. 243-306), except in the following:

1. the future infinitive,
2. present and future participle,
3. supine,
4. gerund and gerundive.

For clarity all the infinitives, participles, gerunds, supines,
and gerundives of the deponents are given in full (pages
72-74).

INFINITIVE

	I	II	III	III (-iō)	IV
336			**Present Tense**		
			(PASSIVE in form; ACTIVE in meaning)		
	hortārī, *to exhort*	verērī, *to fear*	sequī, *to follow*	patī, *to suffer*	mōlīrī, *to set in motion*
337			**Perfect Tense**		
			(PASSIVE in form; ACTIVE in meaning)		
	hortātus, a, um esse, *to have exhorted*	veritus, a, um esse, *to have feared*	secūtus, a, um esse, *to have followed*	passus, a, um esse, *to have suffered*	mōlitus, a, um esse, *to have set in motion*
338			**Future Tense**		
			(ACTIVE IN FORM AND MEANING!)		
	hortātūrus, a, um esse, *to be about to exhort*	veritūrus, a, um esse, *to be about to fear*	secūtūrus, a, um esse, *to be about to follow*	passūrus, a, um esse, *to be about to suffer*	mōlitūrus, a, um esse, *to be about to set in motion*

PARTICIPLE

	I	II	III	III (-iō)	IV

339 — Present Tense
(ACTIVE IN FORM AND MEANING!)

	I	II	III	III (-iō)	IV
	hortāns (hortant-is) *exhorting*	verēns (verent-is) *fearing*	sequēns (sequent-is) *following*	patiēns (patient-is) *suffering*	mōliēns (mōlient-is) *setting in motion*

340 — Future Tense
(ACTIVE IN FORM AND MEANING!)

	I	II	III	III (-iō)	IV
	hortātūrus, a, um *being about to exhort* *about to exhort* *on the point of exhorting*	veritūrus, a, um *being about to fear* *about to fear* *on the point of fearing*	secūtūrus, a, um *being about to follow* *about to follow* *on the point of following*	passūrus, a, um *being about to suffer* *about to suffer* *on the point of suffering*	mōlitūrus, a, um *being about to set in motion* *about to set in motion* *on the point of setting in motion*

341 — Perfect Tense
(PASSIVE in form; ACTIVE in meaning)

	I	II	III	III (-iō)	IV
	hortātus, a, um *having exhorted*	veritus, a, um *having feared*	secūtus, a, um *having followed*	passus, a, um *having suffered*	mōlitus, a, um *having set in motion*

342

GERUND
(ACTIVE IN FORM AND MEANING!)

I	II	III	III (-iō)	IV
hortandī, of exhorting, etc.	verendī, of fearing, etc.	sequendī, of following, etc.	patiendī, of suffering, etc.	mōliendī, of setting in motion, etc.

343

SUPINE
(ACTIVE IN FORM AND MEANING!)

I	II	III	III (-iō)	IV
hortātum	veritum	secūtum	passum	mōlitum
hortātū	veritū	secūtū	passū	mōlitū

344

GERUNDIVE
(PASSIVE IN FORM AND MEANING!)

I	II	III	III (-iō)	IV
hortandus, a, um (ought) to be exhorted	verendus, a, um (ought) to be feared	sequendus, a, um (ought) to be followed	patiendus, a, um (ought) to be suffered	mōliendus, a, um (ought) to be set in motion

Semi-Deponent Verbs.

345 A few verbs have ACTIVE FORMS in the present, imperfect, and future, and PASSIVE FORMS in the perfect, pluperfect, and future perfect, but ACTIVE MEANINGS in all forms.

audeō, audēre, ausus sum, *2, intr.*	*dare* (ausus sum: *I dared*)
gaudeō, gaudēre, gāvīsus sum, *2, intr.*	*rejoice*
soleō, solēre, solitus sum, *2, intr.*	*am accustomed*
fīdō, fīdere, fīsus sum, *3, intr.*	*trust*

IRREGULAR VERBS

SUM, ESSE, FUĪ,[1] FUTŪRUS, *intr., am, be*

INDICATIVE

346   *Present*   **349**   *Perfect*

S.	sum	*I am*	fu-ī[1]	*I have been, I was*
	es	*you are*	fu-istī	*you have been, you were*
	est	*he, she, it is*	fu-it	*he, she, it has been; he, she, it was*
P.	sumus	*we are*	fu-imus	*we have been, we were*
	estis	*you are*	fu-istis	*you have been, you were*
	sunt	*they are*	fu-ērunt	*they have been, they were*

347   *Imperfect*   **350**   *Pluperfect*

S.	eram	*I was*	fu-eram	*I had been*
	erās	*you were*	fu-erās	*you had been*
	erat	*he, she, it was*	fu-erat	*he, she, it had been*
P.	erāmus	*we were*	fu-erāmus	*we had been*
	erātis	*you were*	fu-erātis	*you had been*
	erant	*they were*	fu-erant	*they had been*

348   *Future*   **351**   *Future Perfect*

S.	erō	*I shall be*	fu-erō	*I shall have been*
	eris	*you will be*	fu-eris	*you will have been*
	erit	*he, she, it will be*	fu-erit	*he, she, it will have been*
P.	erimus	*we shall be*	fu-erimus	*we shall have been*
	eritis	*you will be*	fu-eritis	*you will have been*
	erunt	*they will be*	fu-erint	*they will have been*

---

[1]Note that the tenses of the perfect system are formed regularly on **the** perfect stem *fu-*.

SUBJUNCTIVE

352   *Present*   **354**   *Perfect*

S.	sim	*I may be*	fu-erim	*I may have been*
	sīs	*you may be*	fu-erīs	*you may have been*
	sit	*he, she, it may be*	fu-erit	*he, she, it may have been*

P.	sīmus	*we may be*	fu-erīmus	*we may have been*
	sītis	*you may be*	fu-erītis	*you may have been*
	sint	*they may be*	fu-erint	*they may have been*

353   *Imperfect*   **355**   *Pluperfect*

S.	essem	*I might be*	fu-issem	*I might have been*
	essēs	*you might be*	fu-issēs	*you might have been*
	esset	*he, she, it might be*	fu-isset	*he, she, it might have been*

P.	essēmus	*we might be*	fu-issēmus	*we might have been*
	essētis	*you might be*	fu-issētis	*you might have been*
	essent	*they might be*	fu-issent	*they might have been*

IMPERATIVE

356 S.	es	*be*	**357** P.	este	*be*
	estō	*you shall be*		estōte	*you shall be*
	estō	*he shall be*		suntō	*they shall be*

INFINITIVE

358 *Pres.*   esse   *to be*   **359** *Perf.*   fu-isse   *to have been*

360 *Fut.*   { futūrus, a, um esse
fore[1] }   *to be about to be*

PARTICIPLE

361 *Fut.*   futūrus, a, um   *(being) about to be*

---

[1] *Fore* remains unchanged in all genders and numbers.

EŌ, ĪRE, ĪVĪ(IĪ), ITUM, *intr., go.*
FĪŌ, FIERĪ, FACTUS SUM, *intr., am made, become, am done.*
FERŌ, FERRE, TULĪ, LĀTUS, *tr., bear, carry, endure.*

362 Note: All the tenses not shown here are formed regularly.

INDICATIVE

Present Tense

		Active		Passive
	go	*become*	*bear*	
363 S.	eō	**366** fīō	**369** ferō	**372** feror
	īs	fīs	fers	ferris
	it	fit	fert	fertur
P.	īmus	fīmus	ferimus	ferimur
	ītis	fītis	fertis	feriminī
	eunt	fīunt	ferunt	feruntur

Imperfect Tense

364 S.	ībam	**367** fīēbam	**370** ferēbam	**373** ferēbar
	ībās	fīēbās	ferēbās	ferēbāris
	ībat	fīēbat	ferēbat	ferēbātur
P.	ībāmus	fīēbāmus	ferēbāmus	ferēbāmur
	ībātis	fīēbātis	ferēbātis	ferēbāminī
	ībant	fīēbant	ferēbant	ferēbantur

Future Tense

365 S.	ībō	**368** fīam	**371** feram	**374** ferar
	ībis	fīēs	ferēs	ferēris
	ībit	fīet	feret	ferētur
P.	ībimus	fīēmus	ferēmus	ferēmur
	ībitis	fīētis	ferētis	ferēminī
	ībunt	fīent	ferent	ferentur

SUBJUNCTIVE

Present Tense

				Active		Passive
375	⌠ eam	381	fīam	386 feram	392	ferar
S.	⎨ eās		fīās	ferās		ferāris
	⌡ eat		fīat	ferat		ferātur
	⌠ eāmus		fīāmus	ferāmus		ferāmur
P.	⎨ eātis		fīātis	ferātis		ferāminī
	⌡ eant		fīant	ferant		ferantur

Imperfect Tense

				Active		Passive
376	⌠ īrem	382	fierem	387 ferrem	393	ferrer
S.	⎨ īrēs		fierēs	ferrēs		ferrēris
	⌡ īret		fieret	ferret		ferrētur
	⌠ īrēmus		fierēmus	ferrēmus		ferrēmur
P.	⎨ īrētis		fierētis	ferrētis		ferrēminī
	⌡ īrent		fierent	ferrent		ferrentur

IMPERATIVE

377	S. ī	383	fī	388	fer	394	ferre
	P. īte		fīte		ferte		feriminī

INFINITIVE

378	īre	384	fierī	389	ferre	395	ferrī

PARTICIPLE

379	iēns [eunt-is]	....	390	ferēns	....

GERUND

380	eundī, *etc.*	....	391	ferendī, *etc.*	....

GERUNDIVE

....	385	faciendus, a, um	....	396	ferendus, a, um

397   **Eō** has the impersonal passive forms: **ītur, ībātur, itum est, eundum est.** The transitive compounds of **eō** form a full passive by changing the final personal signs; thus: **in-eor, in-īris,** *etc.; infin.,* **in-īrī;** *gerundive,* **ineundus, a, um.**

POSSUM,[1] POSSE, POTUĪ, *intr., can, am able.*
VOLŌ, VELLE, VOLUĪ, *tr., wish, am willing.*
NŌLŌ, NŌLLE, NŌLUĪ, *tr., do not wish, am unwilling.*
MĀLŌ, MĀLLE, MĀLUĪ, *tr., prefer.*

398   Note: All the tenses not shown here are formed regularly.

INDICATIVE

Present Tense

399 S.	possum	402	volō	405	nōlō	408	mālō
	potes		vīs		nōn vīs		māvīs
	potest		vult		nōn vult		māvult
P.	possumus		volumus		nōlumus		mālumus
	potestis		vultis		nōn vultis		māvultis
	possunt		volunt		nōlunt		mālunt

Imperfect Tense

400 S.	poteram	403	volēbam	406	nōlēbam	409	mālēbam
	poterās		volēbās		nōlēbās		mālēbās
	poterat		volēbat		nōlēbat		mālēbat
P.	poterāmus		volēbāmus		nōlēbāmus		mālēbāmus
	poterātis		volēbātis		nōlēbātis		mālēbātis
	poterant		volēbant		nōlēbant		mālēbant

Future Tense

401 S.	poterō	404	volam	407	nōlam	410	mālam
	poteris		volēs		nōlēs		mālēs
	poterit		volet		nōlet		mālet
P.	poterimus		volēmus		nōlēmus		mālēmus
	poteritis		volētis		nōlētis		mālētis
	poterunt		volent		nōlent		mālent

---

[1]The present, imperfect, and future indicative and the present subjunctive consist in a prefix and *sum, es, etc.*
Prefix 'pos' when the next letter will be 's'; *e. g.,* 'pos *sum*' written
possum.
Prefix po*t* when the next letter will be 'e'; *e. g.,* 'pot *es*' written *potes.*

SUBJUNCTIVE

Present Tense

411 S.	velim 414	nōlim 419	mālim 425
possim	velim	nōlim	mālim
possīs	velīs	nōlīs	mālīs
possit	velit	nōlit	mālit

P.			
possīmus	velīmus	nōlīmus	mālīmus
possītis	velītis	nōlītis	mālītis
possint	velint	nōlint	mālint

Imperfect Tense

412 S.	415	420	426
possem	vellem	nōllem	māllem
possēs	vellēs	nōllēs	māllēs
posset	vellet	nōllet	māllet

P.			
possēmus	vellēmus	nōllēmus	māllēmus
possētis	vellētis	nōllētis	māllētis
possent	vellent	nōllent	māllent

IMPERATIVE

S.	....	....	421 nōlī	....
P.	....	....	nōlīte	....

INFINITIVE

413 posse   416 velle   422 nōlle   427 mālle

PARTICIPLE

....	417 volēns	423 nōlēns	428 mālēns
....	(volent-is)	(nōlent-is)	(mālent-is)

GERUND

....   418 volendī, *etc.* 424 nōlendī, *etc.* 429 **mālendī,** *etc.*

COEPĪ,[1] COEPISSE, COEPTUS, *tr., have begun.*
MEMINĪ, MEMINISSE, *tr., remember.*
ŌDĪ, ŌDISSE, ŌSUS, *tr., hate.*

INDICATIVE

Perfect Tense

430 *I began*
coepī, *etc.*

436 *I remember*
meminī, *etc.*

443 *I hate*
ōdī, *etc.*

Pluperfect Tense

431 *I had begun*
coeperam, *etc.*

437 *I remembered*
memineram, *etc.*

444 *I hated*
ōderam, *etc.*

Future Perfect Tense

432 *I shall have begun*
coeperō, *etc.*

438 *I shall remember*
meminerō, *etc.*

445 *I shall hate*
ōderō, *etc.*

SUBJUNCTIVE

Perfect Tense

433 coeperim, *etc.*

439 meminerim, *etc.*

446 ōderim, *etc.*

Pluperfect Tense

434 coepissem, *etc.*

440 meminissem, *etc.*

447 ōdissem, *etc.*

IMPERATIVE

441 *remember*
mementō, -tōte

INFINITIVE

435 *to have begun*
coepisse

442 *to remember*
meminisse

448 *to hate*
ōdisse

---

[1]When *coepī* governs a passive infinitive it is changed to the passive form, *coeptus sum.* It is, however, translated as active. Thus: *Eum laudāre coepī,* "I began to praise him," but: *Urbs aedificārī coepta est,* "The city began to be built."

PARTICIPLE
Future Tense

449 *about to begin*   ....   451 *about to hate*
coeptūrus, a, um   ....   ōsūrus, a, um

Perfect Tense

450 *begun*   ....
coeptus, a, um   ....

INQUAM, *I say.*

Present Tense
452 inquam inquis   inquit   inquimus   .... inquiunt

Imperfect Tense
453 .... inquiēbat ....

Future Tense
454 .... inquiēs inquiet ....

Perfect Tense
455 .... inquistī inquit ....

AJŌ, *I say.*

Present Tense
456 ajō   ais   ait   .... ajunt

Imperfect Tense
457 ajēbam ajēbās   ajēbat   ajēbāmus   ajēbātis   ajēbant

Present Subjunctive
458 .... ajās   ajat   .... ajant

QUAESŌ, *I beg, I entreat.*

Present Indicative Active
459 quaesō .... quaesumus ....

PART 2

SYNTAX

ORDER OF WORDS

460   **The verb is last.**

Caesar Gallum interfēcit.
Caesar killed a Gaul.

Caesar, etsī in hīs locīs hiemēs mātūrae sunt, in Britanniam proficīscī contendit.
Although the winters in these regions are early, Caesar hastened to set out for Britain.

Note:

461   1. Forms of the verb **sum,** *am,* may stand anywhere in the sentence.

Deus est bonus.
Deus bonus est.
God is good.

462   2. The imperative more frequently stands first.

Pugnāte, mīlitēs, fortiter.
Fight bravely, soldiers.

463   3. The vocative generally does not stand first.

Pugnāte, mīlitēs, fortiter.
Soldiers! fight bravely.

464   Adjectives of *quantity*, *size*, and *number*,
demonstrative and *interrogative* adjectives
stand BEFORE the nouns they modify.

> Multī hominēs
> *Many men*
>
> Trēs et vīgintī nautae
> *Twenty-three sailors*
>
> Hic vir
> *This man*
>
> Quem in locum?
> *Into which place?*

465   Adjectives of *quality*
and *possessive* adjectives
stand AFTER the nouns they modify.

> Vir bonus
> *A good man*
>
> Pater meus
> *My father*

466   *Adverbs* and *ablatives*
stand BEFORE the verbs and adjectives they modify.

> Equitēs celeriter vēnērunt.
> *The cavalry came swiftly.*
>
> Laude dignus
> *Worthy of praise*

467   Temporal clauses,
the ablative absolute,
conditional and concessive clauses
PRECEDE the main clause.
Other clauses, especially result clauses,
FOLLOW the main clause.

> Cum eum dē hāc rē certiōrem fēcissent, abiērunt.
> *When they had informed him of this, they went away.*

> Sī vim faciētis prohibēbō.
> *If you use force, I shall prevent you.*

> Tanta erat tempestās ut nāvēs frangerentur.
> *There was so terrible a storm that the ships were destroyed.*

468   **Note:** Purpose clauses (more) often precede.

> Ut eōs pācāret lēgātum mīsit.
> *He sent a lieutenant to pacify them.*

469   Words are put in unusual positions for emphasis, balance, or other rhetorical effects.

> Aliud iter habēmus nullum.
> *We have no other way.*

RULES OF AGREEMENT

470   A finite verb agrees with its subject in *person* and *number*.

> Deus est.
> *God is.*

Note: With a COMPOUND subject:

471   1. Either the verb is **plural**; the **first** person is preferred to the second, the **second** to the third.

> Ego et tū vēnimus.
> *You and I have come.*
>
> Tū et ille captī estis.
> *You and he have been captured.*

472   2. OR the verb may agree with the nearest, especially when the verb stands before or between the subjects, or when the subjects are things.

> Caesar vēnit et ego.
> *Caesar and I came.*
>
> Tempus necessitāsque postulat.
> *The time and the need demand it.*

473   **A predicate noun agrees with the subject, and an appositive agrees with its noun in *case* (if possible, also in gender and number).**

> Chrīstus Rēx est.
> *Christ is King.*
>
> Nuntius ā Caesare, duce Rōmānōrum, missus est.
> *The message was sent by Caesar, the leader of the Romans.*

474   **A predicate adjective agrees with its noun in *gender, number,* and *case*.**

> Vīta brevis est.
> *Life is short.*

Note: With more than one subject:

475   1. If **persons** of different sexes, the predicate adjective is **masculine**.

> Pater et fīlia mortuī sunt.
> *Father and daughter are dead.*

476   **2. If things of different genders, the predicate adjective
agrees with the nearest or is neuter.**

        Impedīmenta et equitātus <u>secūtus</u> est.
        The baggage and cavalry followed.
        Castella et vīcī <u>dēlēta</u> sunt.
        The forts and the villages were destroyed.

477   **An attributive adjective agrees with its noun
in *gender*, *number*, and *case*.**

      Mīles <u>fortis</u> pugnat.
      The <u>brave</u> soldier fights.

478   **Note:** With more than one word the attributive adjective
          agrees with the nearest or is repeated with each.

        Multī patrēs et fīliae
        Patrēs et fīliae multae
        Multī patrēs et multae fīliae
        Many fathers and daughters

479   **A pronoun agrees with the word to which it refers,
in *gender* and *number*;
its *case* depends on its use in its own clause.**

      Rōma est magna urbs. Vīdistīne <u>eam</u>?
      Rome is a large city. Have you seen it?

      Contrā Germānōs exercitum dūxit. <u>Hī</u> sunt fortēs.
      He led his army against the Germans. These are brave.

      Marīa <u>quam</u> laudāmus Māter Deī est.
      Mary, whom we praise, is the Mother of God.

MAIN CLAUSES

USE OF THE TENSES OF THE INDICATIVE

480   The action or state expressed by a verb has stage and time.

     Stage: The action or state may be beginning, continuing, or completed.

     Time: The action or state may be present, past, or future.

481   **Note:** In theory, therefore, nine different forms of the verb are possible in the indicative: three forms—representing the three different stages—for each of the three times. Actually, however, languages are more economical, using one form for two or more stages or times. Thus the present indicative in Latin represents the stages of beginning and continuing in present time. The precise meaning of such forms is indicated by the context.

482   The following chart shows the different stages and times expressed by the tenses of the Latin indicative:

TIME

		Present	Future	Past
S T A G E	*Beginning*	*present tense* laudō I (begin to) praise	*future tense* laudābō I shall (begin to) praise	*historical perfect* laudāvī I praised (began to praise)
	Continuing	*present tense* laudō I am praising	*future tense* laudābō I shall be praising	*imperfect* laudābam I was praising
	Completed	*present perfect* laudāvī I have praised	*future perfect* laudāverō I shall have praised	*pluperfect* laudāveram I had praised

The present tense expresses an action or state as:

483　1. Begun, continued, or repeated in present time.

Hūjus cīvitātis est longē amplissima auctōritās.
The influence of this nation is by far the greatest.

Jam diū mortem nostram cupis.
You have long (since) been desiring our death.

484　2. Universally true.

Omnēs hominēs lībertātī student.
Everyone is eager for liberty.

485　3. Happening in past time; the past is put before our eyes
as happening now *(historical present)*.

Circumsistunt hominem atque interficiunt.
They surrounded the fellow and killed him.
(They surround him and kill him.)

The imperfect tense expresses an action or state as:

486　1. Begun, continued, or repeated (habitual) in past time.

Nostra classis ūnā celeritāte praestābat.
Our fleet was superior in point of speed alone.

Jam prīdem mortem nostram cupiēbās.
You had long (since) been desiring our death.

487　2. Happening at the same time as other past actions or
states. It is, therefore, the *descriptive* tense of past time.

Etsī hostēs oppugnābant, nostrī nōn timēbant.
*Although the enemy were attacking, our men were not
afraid.*

488　3. Attempted in past time.

Eī persuādēbat ut ā Caesare dēficeret.
He was trying to persuade him to revolt against Caesar.
(i. e., he was unsuccessfully attempting to persuade.)

The future tense expresses an action or state as:

489   1. Begun, continued, or repeated in future time.

Quā laetitiā perfruēris!
What pleasure will you enjoy!

490   2. As generally true.

Ut sēmentem fēceris, ita metēs.
As you sow, so shall you reap.

491   **Note:** The future is sometimes equivalent to a command.

Hunc ā vītā cīvium arcēbis!
Ward this man off from the lives of our citizens!
(You will ward this man off from the lives of our citi-
zens!)

The perfect tense expresses an action or state as:

492   1. Done in past time *(historical perfect)*. It is, therefore, the *narrative* tense of past time.

Subitum autem bellum in Galliā coortum est.
A sudden war, however, broke out in Gaul.

493   2. Completed in present time *(present perfect)*.

Vēnī.
I have come.
(The act of *coming* is *now* completed.)

The pluperfect tense expresses an action or state as:

494   1. Completed in past time.

Venetōrum nāvēs ad hunc modum factae erant.
The ships of the Veneti had been (were) built in this
way.
(The act of *building* was *then* completed.)

495　　2. Completed before another past act or state.

> Nāvēs eōdem unde erant profectae revertērunt.
> *The ships returned to the same place from which they had set out.*
> (The *setting out* was before the past act of *returning*.)

The future perfect tense expresses an action or state as:

496　　1. Completed in future time.

> Hoc cūrāverō.
> *This shall be my care.*

497　　2. Completed before another future act or state.

> Ut sēmentem fēceris, ita metēs.
> *As you sow (will have sown), so shall you reap.*
> (The *sowing* will be completed before the future act of *reaping*.)

KINDS OF MAIN CLAUSES

STATEMENTS

498   **Statements of fact are expressed in the indicative; negative:** *nōn.*

> Gallia est omnis dīvīsa in partēs trēs.
> *Gaul taken as a whole is divided into three parts.*

Note:

499   1. The **present infinitive** is sometimes used in place of the **imperfect indicative** for vividness *(historical infinitive)*.

> Nostrī fortiter repugnāre.
> *Our men were resisting vigorously.*

500   2. To state a modest judgment or a simple possibility the subjunctive is used, the present and perfect for present time, the imperfect for past time *(potential subjunctive)*.

> Velim (nōlim, mālim).
> *I should like (not like, prefer).*

> Dīxerit aliquis.
> *Someone may say.*

> Vidērēs (cernerēs, putārēs).
> *You might have seen (observed, thought).*

501   3. In the potential subjunctive the second person singular and the third person plural are usually **indefinite**.

> Crēderēs.
> *One*
> *You*   *might have thought.*
> *A person*

DIRECT QUESTIONS

502   **DEFINITION:** A direct question is one addressed directly to someone, and which uses the exact words of the original speaker.

Quis es? *Who are you?*

Centuriō, "Quis," inquit, "vēnit?"
The centurion said, "Who came?"

503   Direct questions are introduced by:

1. interrogative pronouns, adjectives, and adverbs.
2. *nōnne* if the answer 'yes' is expected.
3. *num* { if the answer 'no' is expected.
             { to express surprise.
4. *-ne*   to ask for information.
            (Add *-ne* to the emphatic word and put first in the sentence.)

Pronoun: Quis es? *Who are you?*

Adjective: Quam urbem oppugnāvērunt?
                 Which city did they attack?

Adverb: Ubi sunt? *Where are they?*

Nōnne: Nōnne Deus est bonus?
                God is good, isn't He?
                Isn't God good? (Answer: 'yes.')

Num: Num Caesar victus est?
                Caesar wasn't conquered, was he?
                Surely Caesar wasn't conquered?
                (Answer: 'no.')

-Ne: Vīdistīne Rōmam?
                Have you seen Rome?
                (Answer: *"I have seen Rome"* or *"I have not seen Rome"*; 'yes' or 'no.')

Note:

1. DOUBLE QUESTIONS:

504   **Definition:** A double question is one that gives two alternatives:

         (1)   (2)
         Will you fight or will you flee?

505   **Direct double questions are introduced by:**

     1. utrum . . . . an
     2. -ne . . . . . . an
     3. . . . . an
         (. . . *'or not'* is **annōn**)

         Will you fight or will you flee?
         Utrum pugnābis an fugiēs?
         Pugnābisne an fugiēs?
         Pugnābis an fugiēs?

         Will you fight or not?
         Utrum pugnābis annōn?
         Pugnābisne annōn?
         Pugnābis annōn?

506   2. Sometimes no introductory word is used, especially when the question is asked in surprise.

         Vōcis exspectās contumēliam?
         Are you waiting for a spoken attack?

   3. **An** sometimes introduces single questions:

507   a. When a preceding member is easily understood.

         Mōsne mājōrum impedit? An lēgēs?
         Do our traditions prevent it? Or do the laws?

508   b. Implying a negative answer.

         An dubitāmus?
         Or do we doubt it? (Absurd!)

DELIBERATIVE QUESTIONS

509 **DEFINITION:** A deliberative question is one asked in doubt or indignation about a course of action (what is or was to be done).

510 **A deliberative question is put in the subjunctive;**
present for present time;
imperfect for past time;
negative: *nōn*.

  PRESENT TIME : Quid faciam?
        What should I do?
        What am I to do?

        Hunc ego nōn dīligam?
        Should I not love this man?

  PAST TIME : Quid facerent?
        What were they to do?

        Pecūniam nōn trāderem?
        Was I not to hand over the money?

WISHES

511 1. **POSSIBLE wishes are expressed by the**
   PRESENT SUBJUNCTIVE with *UTINAM*.
   (With the third person *utinam* is often omitted.)
   Negative: *nē*.

    (Utinam) nostrī vincant!
    May our men conquer!

    (The battle is still going on; neither side has conquered as yet; it is still POSSIBLE for this wish to come true. Note that the English translation requires the auxiliary verb 'may.' **Utinam** is not translated.)

    Nē veniant.
    May they not come.

512 2. Wishes CONTRARY TO A PRESENT FACT
are expressed by the
IMPERFECT SUBJUNCTIVE with *UTINAM*.
Negative: *nē*.

> Utinam Caesar vīveret.
> *Would that Caesar were living.*
>
> (The FACT is that Caesar is NOW dead; the wish is
> CONTRARY TO A PRESENT FACT. Note that the
> English is 'would that' and uses the English auxiliary
> verb 'were' or 'was.')
>
> Utinam nē adesset.
> *Would that he was (were) not present.*

513 3. Wishes CONTRARY TO A PAST FACT
are expressed by the
PLUPERFECT SUBJUNCTIVE with *UTINAM*.
Negative: *nē*.

> Utinam Pīlātus Chrīstum dēfendisset.
> *Would that Pilate had defended Christ.*
>
> (As a matter of FACT Pilate did NOT defend Christ.
> The wish is CONTRARY TO A PAST FACT. Note
> that the English uses the PLUPERFECT INDICA-
> TIVE.)
>
> Utinam nē Chrīstum occīdissent.
> *Would that they had not killed Christ.*

JUSSIVE SUBJUNCTIVE

514 Commands in the third person (he, she, it, they)
are expressed by the PRESENT SUBJUNCTIVE.
Negative: *nē*.

Impetum faciant.
Let them make an attack.

Nē pugnet.
Let him not fight.

COMMANDS IN THE SECOND PERSON

In the second person:

515 1. Positive commands are expressed by the imperative,
usually in the present tense.

Pugnāte fortiter.
Fight bravely.

516 2. For negative commands use:

a. *nōlī* ('be unwilling to') with the INFINITIVE.

Nōlī pugnāre.
Do not fight.

b. *nē* with the PERFECT SUBJUNCTIVE.

Nē crēdiderīs.
Do not believe it.

c. *cavē* ('beware') or *vidē* ('see to it') with *nē* and
the PRESENT SUBJUNCTIVE.

Cavē nē timeās.
Do not be afraid.

517 Note: The second person **present** subjunctive is used in
commands (negative: *nē*) when the subject is **indefinite** and **general** or in very **familiar** speech.

Quidquid agis, prūdenter agās.
Whatever you do, do it wisely.

HORTATORY SUBJUNCTIVE

518 An exhortation in the first person plural is expressed
by the PRESENT SUBJUNCTIVE.
Negative: *nē.*

> Pugnēmus.
> *Let us fight.*

> Nē cēdāmus.
> *Let us not yield.*

> (Note that English uses the verb 'let' and puts the **person**
> in the **accusative**; the Latin makes the **person** the **sub-
> ject** of the main verb.)

CONCESSIVE SUBJUNCTIVE

519 The subjunctive, sometimes preceded by *ut,*
is used to show that something is 'granted' or 'conceded.'
Present tense for present time;
perfect tense for past time;
negative: *nē.*

PRESENT TIME: Sit vērum.
                Granted that it is true.
                I grant that it is true.
                (Lit.: *Let it be true.*)

                Ut ita sit.
                Granted that it is so.

PAST TIME: Nē fuerit fortis.
                Granted that he was not brave.
                I grant that he was not brave.
                Suppose he was not brave.

SUBORDINATE CLAUSES

TENSES IN SUBORDINATE CLAUSES

520 Tenses in subordinate clauses are generally determined by one of the following principles (Nos. 521-545). The particular rules for the various subordinate clauses (purpose clauses, temporal clauses, *etc.*) will indicate in each case which principle is to be followed (*e. g.*, see No. 550).

1. TENSE BY SENSE

521 **The tenses of the indicative have the same meanings as in simple sentences.**

> Legiōnēs quās nūper cōnscrīpserat aderant.
> *The legions which he had recently enrolled were present.*

522 **The tenses of the subjunctive have the same meanings as the corresponding tenses of the indicative.**

523 **Note:** However, the Latin, in general, is more careful than the English in marking relations of time.

> Cum Rōmam vēnerō, tē vidēbō.
> *When I come to Rome, I shall see you.*
> (The 'coming' is before the 'seeing'; therefore, the future perfect is used.)

2. TENSE BY SEQUENCE

The tense in many subordinate **SUBJUNCTIVE** clauses is determined by the rules for the **SEQUENCE OF TENSES.**

524 **Primary and Secondary Tenses.** The tenses of the indicative and subjunctive are divided into two groups:

INDICATIVE		SUBJUNCTIVE
Present Future Future Perfect	These are PRIMARY tenses	Present Perfect
Imperfect Perfect Pluperfect	These are SECONDARY tenses	Imperfect Pluperfect

525 **Primary Sequence.**

When the verb in the main clause is a **PRIMARY TENSE,** the verb in the subordinate clause must be a **PRIMARY** tense.

Rogō quis veniat. *I ask who is coming.*

Rogābō quis veniat. *I shall ask who is coming.*

Rogāverō quis veniat. *I shall have asked who is coming.*

526 **Secondary Sequence.**

When the verb in the main clause is a **SECONDARY TENSE,** the verb in the subordinate clause must be a **SECONDARY** tense.

Rogāvī quis essēs. *I asked who you were.*

Rogābam quis essēs. *I was asking who you were.*

Rogāveram quis essēs. *I had asked who you were.*

In Primary Sequence:

527   1. **When the action of the subordinate verb happens BEFORE the action of the main verb, the PERFECT subjunctive must be used.**

Rogō quis vēnerit.   *I ask who came.*
Rogābō quis vēnerit.   *I shall ask who came.*
Rogāverō quis vēnerit. *I shall have asked who came.*

(In all these sentences the action of 'coming' happens before the action of 'asking.')

528   2. **When the action of the subordinate verb happens AT THE SAME TIME AS the action of the main verb, the PRESENT subjunctive must be used.**

Rogō quid videās.   *I ask what you see.*
Rogābō quid videās.   *I shall ask what you are seeing.*
Rogāverō quid videās. *I shall have asked what you are seeing.*

(In all these sentences the action of 'seeing' happens at the same time as the action of 'asking.')

529   3. **When the action of the subordinate verb WILL HAPPEN AFTER the action of the main verb the PRESENT subjunctive must be used.**

Veniō ut videam. *I am coming to see.*
(The 'seeing' will happen after the 'coming.')

530   **Note:** But in indirect questions and **quīn**-clauses, sometimes in result clauses and other clauses (especially for clarity or emphasis), the future participle active (**-ūrus, a, um**) is used as a predicate adjective with the present subjunctive of **sum** (**sim**, *etc.*).

Rogō quis ventūrus sit. *I ask who* { *will come.*
is about to come.
is going to come. }

In Secondary Sequence:

531 1. When the action of the subordinate verb happens BEFORE the action of the main verb, the PLU-PERFECT subjunctive must be used.

> Rogāvī quis advēnisset. *I asked who had come.*
> (The 'coming' happened before the 'asking.')

532 2. When the action of the subordinate verb happens AT THE SAME TIME AS the action of the main verb, the IMPERFECT subjunctive must be used in the subordinate clause.

> Rogāvī quis pugnāret.   *I asked who was fighting.*
> (The 'fighting' happens at the same time as the 'asking.')

533 3. When the action of the subordinate verb happens AFTER the action of the main verb, the IMPER-FECT subjunctive must be used.

> Vēnit ut urbem oppugnāret.
> *He came to attack the city.*
> (The 'attacking' happens after the 'coming.')

534 Note: In indirect questions and quīn-clauses, sometimes in result clauses and other clauses (especially for clarity or emphasis), the future participle active (-ūrus, a, um) is used as a predicate adjective with the imperfect of **sum** (**essem**, *etc.*)

> Rogāvī quis ventūrus esset.
>
> *I asked* { *who was going to come.*
> *who would come.*
> *who was about to come.* }

535   SUMMARY DIAGRAM

The vertical line represents the TIME of the ACTION OF THE MAIN VERB. At the top of this line the primary or secondary tenses of the indicative are shown. The horizontal line represents the time of the action of the subordinate clause. The required tenses of the subjunctive are indicated for the three times possible: (1) before the main action, (2) at the same time as the main action, (3) after (future to) the main action. Understand and memorize this outline. It will enable you to explain any tense by sequence.

536   PRIMARY SEQUENCE:

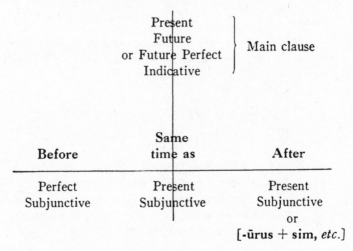

537   **SECONDARY SEQUENCE:**

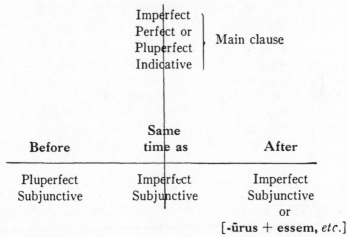

Imperfect
Perfect or   } Main clause
Pluperfect
Indicative

Before	Same time as	After
Pluperfect Subjunctive	Imperfect Subjunctive	Imperfect Subjunctive or [**-ūrus + essem,** *etc.*]

Note:

538   1. A subjunctive dependent on a SUBORDINATE infinitive, supine, gerund, gerundive, participle, or subjunctive takes its sequence not from one of these but from the MAIN VERB.

> Cōnstituī ad tē venīre ut tē vidērem.
> *I determined to come to you to see you.*

(The subjunctive **vidērem** depends on the PRESENT infinitive **venīre** but is in secondary sequence because of the main verb, **cōnstituī**.)

539   2. However, a subjunctive dependent on a SUBORDINATE PERFECT SUBJUNCTIVE OR A PERFECT INFINITIVE is usually in SECONDARY SEQUENCE, regardless of the main verb.

> Videor multa verba fēcisse ut tibi persuādērem.
> *I seem to have spoken at great length to persuade you.*

(**Persuādērem** depends on the perfect infinitive **fēcisse** and is therefore SECONDARY despite the PRIMARY main verb **videor.**)

540   3. The present perfect *(e. g.,* vēnī, *I HAVE come)* generally takes secondary, sometimes primary, sequence.

> Vēnī ut tēcum loquar.
> *I have come to speak with you.*

541   4. The historical present may take either sequence.

> Mandat ut quam prīmum $\begin{cases} \text{revertātur.} \\ \text{reverterētur.} \end{cases}$

> *He instructed him to return at the earliest possible moment.*

> (**Mandat** is the present indicative but is used **in context** of a **past** action for vividness. See No. 485.)

3. TENSES IN STATEMENTS OF GENERAL TRUTHS OR REPEATED ACTION

542   Complex sentences which express a GENERAL truth or REPEATED action regularly have the INDICATIVE in both main and subordinate clauses. This rule holds when the subordinate clause is introduced by a temporal conjunction (**cum,** *when,* **quandōcumque,** *whenever,* **ubi,** *when, etc.*), a conditional conjunction (**sī,** *if,* **nisi,** *unless*), a relative adverb (**ubi,** *where, etc.*), a relative pronoun (**quī, quae, quod,** *who, what, that,* **quīcumque, quaecumque, quodcumque,** *whoever, whatever, etc.*).

The TENSES are determined by the following rules (Nos. 543-545):

543 1. IN PRESENT TIME:

MAIN clause: PRESENT tense.

SUBORDINATE clause:

1. To express action <u>before</u> the main verb: PER-FECT tense;

2. To express action <u>at the same time</u> as the main verb: PRESENT tense.

> Quandōcumque domum rediī, dormiō.
> *Whenever I come home, I sleep.*
> (I come home BEFORE I sleep; hence, PER-FECT TENSE, **rediī**.)
>
> Quandōcumque hunc librum legō, multum discō.
> *Whenever I read this book, I learn much.*

544 2. IN PAST TIME:

MAIN clause: IMPERFECT tense.

SUBORDINATE clause:

1. To express action <u>before</u> the main verb: PLU-PERFECT tense;

2. To express action <u>at the same time</u> as the main verb: IMPERFECT tense.

> Quandōcumque domum redieram, dormiēbam.
> *Whenever I returned home, I slept.*
> (I returned home BEFORE I slept; hence PLU-PERFECT TENSE, **redieram**.)
>
> Sī hunc librum legēbam, multum discēbam.
> *If (ever) I read this book, I learned much.*

545 3. IN FUTURE TIME:

MAIN clause: FUTURE tense.

SUBORDINATE clause:

1. To express action <u>before</u> the main verb: FUTURE PERFECT tense;

2. To express action <u>at the same time</u> as the main verb: FUTURE tense.

Cum domum <u>redierō, dormiam.</u>
Whenever I come home, I shall sleep.

(I come home BEFORE I sleep; hence, FUTURE PERFECT TENSE, redierō.)

Quīcumque hunc librum <u>leget</u> multum <u>discet.</u>
Whoever reads this book, will learn much.

ADVERBIAL CLAUSES

PURPOSE CLAUSES

546   Purpose clauses are introduced by:
1. *ut* (negative: *nē*),
2. *quī, quae, quod,*[1]
3. *quō* (negative: *nē*) before a comparative;
Mood: subjunctive;
Tense: after a *primary* tense, use the *present;*
      after a *secondary* tense, use the *imperfect.*

Pugnō ut vincam.

I fight
{
to conquer.
in order that I may conquer.
that I may conquer.
in order to conquer.
for the purpose of conquering.
for the sake of conquering.
}

Pugnāvī ut vincerem.

I fought
{
in order that I might conquer.
in order to conquer.
that I might conquer.
to conquer.
for the purpose of conquering.
for the sake of conquering.
}

Pugnō nē vincar.

I fight lest I be conquered.

I fight that I may not be conquered.

---

[1]See No. 625 for purpose clauses introduced by a relative and Nos. 637, 639 for noun clauses of purpose.

Note:

547   1. Quō (negative: nē) is used when the purpose clause contains a **comparative** adverb or adjective.

Urbem mūnīvit quō facilius eam dēfenderet.
He fortified the city that he might more easily defend it.

Mīlitēs in castra vocāvit nē diūtius pugnārent.
He called the soldiers into the camp lest they fight longer.

548   2. *And in order that . . . not* is **nēve (neu).**

549   3. *That no one . . .* is **nē quis** *(lest anyone).*
That never . . . . is **nē umquam** *(lest ever).*
That nothing . . . is **nē quid** *(lest anything).*
That nowhere . . is **nēcubi** *(lest anywhere).*

RESULT CLAUSES

550   Result clauses are introduced by:
1. *ut* (negative: *ut nōn*),
2. *quī, quae, quod;*[1]
subjunctive;
tense by sequence (Nos. 524-537, but see Nos. 554, 555).

Sīc vītam ēgit ut omnēs eum laudārent.
He so lived that everyone praised him.

Sīc vītam ēgit ut multī eum nōn laudārent.
He so lived that many did not praise him.

---

[1]See No. 626 for result clauses introduced by a relative and Nos. 637-638 for noun clauses of result.

Note:

551 1. The main clause usually contains an adverb of degree or manner or a similar adjective:

tālis, e	*such, of such a kind*
tantus, a, um	*so great*
sīc; ita	*so, in such a manner*
tam; adeō	*so, to such a degree, etc.*

552 2. When both the main clause and the result clause are NEGATIVE, **quīn** may be used for **ut nōn.**

Nihil tam difficile est quīn quaerendō invēstīgārī possit.
Nothing is so difficult that it can not be discovered by searching.

553 3. **Quam ut** is used to denote result after COMPARATIVES.

Fortior erat quam ut fugeret.
He was too brave to flee.
(Lit.: *He was braver than that he should flee.* Note that the English regularly uses *too* and the infinitive in such sentences.)

554 4. To emphasize the actual occurrence of a past result or to indicate that the result continues up to the present, the PERFECT is used in SECONDARY sequence.

Hostēs tot erant ut dēvictī sīmus.
The enemy were so numerous that we were (actually) defeated.

555 5. To express the present result of a past action, the PRESENT subjunctive is used in SECONDARY sequence.

Adulēscēns tam strēnuē labōrāvī ut dīves nunc sim.
I worked so hard as a youth that I am now rich.

TEMPORAL CLAUSES

556 *Ut, ubi*   'when'

postquam
posteāquam } 'after'

simul ac
simul atque
ubi prīmum } 'as soon as'
ut prīmum
cum prīmum

when expressing a
single[1] *past* act take
the PERFECT
INDICATIVE.

Ubi Caesarem vīdērunt, lēgātōs ad eum mīsērunt.
When they saw Caesar, they sent envoys to him.

Ut hoc vīdit, equitātum praemīsit.
When he saw this, he sent the cavalry ahead.

Caesar, postquam id vīdit, equitātum praemīsit.
After he had seen this, Caesar sent forward the cavalry.

Simul atque dē Caesaris adventū certiōrēs factī sunt,
fūgērunt.
*As soon as they were informed of the arrival of Caesar,
they fled.*

Note:

557 1. Even where the English has the PLUPERFECT, these
conjunctions generally take the PERFECT.

> *When Caesar had seen this, he sent the cavalry ahead.*
> Caesar, ubi hoc vīdit, equitātum praemīsit.

---

[1]When expressing repeated action, these clauses follow the rules given in
No. 544.

558 2. If the interval of time (after which) is expressed, however, **postquam** regularly takes the pluperfect.

> Tertiō diē postquam vēnerat eum vīdī.
> (or: Tertiō post diē quam, *etc.*)
> *I saw him on the third day after he came.*

559 *CUM,* 'when,' when referring to PRESENT or FUTURE time takes the INDICATIVE;
TENSE BY SENSE (Nos. 521-523).

> Cum adest, nihil timēmus.
> *When he is present, we fear nothing.*
>
> Cum nōn erō, quid sentiam?
> *When I shall not exist, what shall I feel?*
>
> Cum in Galliam pervēnerō, pācem vōbīscum faciam.
> *When I come (shall have come) to Gaul, I shall make peace with you.*

CUM, 'when,' when referring to PAST time:

560 1. If it sets the point of time (usually *tum, eō tempore* or a similar expression is found in the main clause): INDICATIVE;
TENSE BY SENSE (Nos. 521-523).

> Tum, cum haec gerēbantur, Caesar in Galliā erat.
> *At the time when these things were happening, Caesar was in Gaul.*

561　2. **If it describes the circumstances:**
SUBJUNCTIVE;
TENSE BY SEQUENCE (Nos. 524-537).

Cum equitēs in silvīs <u>pugnārent,</u> Caesar mīlitēs (trāns) flūmen trādūxit.
When the cavalry <u>were fighting</u> in the forest, Caesar led the troops across the river.

Caesar, cum hostēs <u>vīdisset,</u> legiōnēs prō castrīs īnstrūxit.
When Caesar <u>had seen</u> the enemy, he drew up the legions in front of the camp.

Note:

562　1. In some sentences the main action is put in the **cum**-clause. The imperfect or pluperfect indicative is then used in the main clause, and the perfect or historical present indicative in the **cum**-clause *(cum inversum).*

Hostēs jam oppugnābant, cum subitō vīsus est Caesar.
The enemy were already attacking, when suddenly Caesar appeared.
(The main action is the appearance of Caesar.)
Vix dīxerat, cum mīles cecidit (cadit) in terram.
The soldier had just spoken, when he fell to the ground.

563　2. When expressing REPEATED action, **cum**-clauses follow the rules given in Nos. 542-545.

Dum (dōnec), quoad,   'until'   ⎫
antequam, anteāquam, priusquam,   'before' ⎬ take:
                                                ⎭

564   1. **The indicative when the subordinate action merely follows the main action (the subordinate clause simply states an *actual fact*).**

> Ē vītā excessit antequam sōl ortus est.
> *He died before the sun rose.*
> (It happened that the sun rose after his death. Merely the FACT is stated.)

Note:

565   1. The subjunctive *may* be used even in this case with **antequam, anteāquam,** and **priusquam,** but generally the indicative is used.

566   2. Generally only the present, perfect, and future perfect indicative are used; instead of the pluperfect, the perfect is used; instead of the future, the present.

   2. **The subjunctive; tense by sequence (Nos. 524-537):**

567   a. **when the agent of the main action *anticipates (intends, acts to prevent)* the subordinate action.**

> Horātius impetum hostium sustinuit, quoad cēterī pontem <u>interrumperent.</u>
> *Horatius held off the enemy until the others should break down the bridge.*
> (Horatius deliberately held off the enemy so that the others could break down the bridge.)

568   b. **when the subordinate action is merely *possible*.**

> Priusquam satis certa cōnsilia <u>essent,</u> alia clādēs nuntiātur.
> *Before very definite plans could be formed, another disaster was reported.*
> (The subordinate clause states a *possibility*.)

Dum, 'while,' 'as long as':

569   1. If the time of the *dum*-clause is LONGER than the
time of the main clause, the PRESENT indicative is
always used in the *dum*-clause.

Dum in hortō sedeō, vulnerātus sum.

While I was sitting in the garden, I was wounded.

In this diagram the solid (horizontal) line represents
the duration of the time in the **dum**-clause. The dotted
(vertical) line represents the time at which the wounding
occurred.

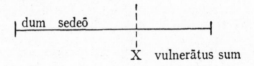

570   2. If the time of the two clauses is of the SAME
LENGTH, the indicative and the SAME TENSE as
that in the main clause is used in the *dum*-clause.

Dum in hortō sedēbam, legēbam.

While (i.e., *as long as*) *I was sitting in the garden,
I read (was reading).*

In this diagram the solid horizontal lines represent the
length of time in the two clauses.

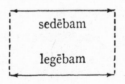

571   Note: **Quoad** and **quamdiū**, *as long as,* follow the second
rule (No. 570) for **dum.**

CAUSAL CLAUSES

Quod, quia, quoniam, 'because,' take:

572   1. The INDICATIVE when the reason is given as the real reason (i. e., the reason is an objective fact and the writer is willing to take responsibility for its being the real reason).

> Quod mīles fortis nōn fuit, fūgit.
> *Because the soldier was not brave, he fled.*
> (The soldier was actually a coward. That is the reason for his fleeing, and the writer or speaker is willing to vouch for its truth.)

573   2. The SUBJUNCTIVE (TENSE BY SEQUENCE, Nos. 524-537) when the reason is given as the reason alleged (i. e., the reason may or may not be an objective fact, but it is the reason that people other than the speaker or writer give for the action in the main clause).

> Quod mīles fortis nōn fuisset, fūgit.
> *Because the soldier was not brave, he fled.*
> (The soldier may or may not have been brave, but people other than the writer give that as the reason for his fleeing.)

> Imperātor lēgātum laudat quod fortiter pugnāverit.
> *The commander praises the lieutenant because he fought bravely.*
> (The lieutenant may or may not have fought bravely, but that is the commander's reason for praising him.)

Note:

574   1. The REJECTED REASON is expressed by
nōn quod or nōn quō, *not because,*
with the subjunctive
(tense by sequence, Nos. 524-537).

> Eam amō nōn quod pulchra sit sed quod bona est.
> *I love her NOT BECAUSE SHE IS BEAUTIFUL but be-*
> *cause she is good.*
> (**Nōn quod pulchra sit** is the *rejected reason.*)

575   **Note:** If the rejected reason is a FACT, the indicative
may be used.

> Eam amō nōn quod pulchra est sed quod bona est.
> *I love her NOT BECAUSE SHE IS BEAUTIFUL*
> *but because she is good.*
> (It is a *fact* that she is beautiful, but that is *not my*
> *reason* for loving her.)

576   2. After verbs meaning *praise, blame, accuse, admire,* and
the like, the subjunctive construction is generally used.

> Laudat Africānum quod <u>fuerit</u> abstinēns.
> *He praises Africanus for having been self-controlled.*
> (Lit.: *because he was self-controlled.*)

577   3. Quandō, sīquidem, quandōquidem, *seeing that, inas-*
much as, take the indicative.

> Id omittō, quandō vōbīs ita <u>placet</u>.
> *I pass that over, seeing that you so wish.*

578   *Cum,* 'since,'
takes the subjunctive;
tense by sequence (Nos. 524-537).[1]

> Quae cum ita sint, discēde!
> *Since this is the case, depart!*

---

[1]See No. 627 for causal clauses introduced by a relative.

579   With verbs of emotion[1] the reason is expressed by:

1. *quod:* subjunctive; tense by sequence (Nos. 524-537).

2. *quod:* indicative; tense by sense (Nos. 521-523).

3. accusative with the infinitive; tense by relation (Nos. 885-887).

> Gaudeō quod vēnerīs.
> *I am glad that you (should) have come.*

> Gaudeō quod vēnistī.
> *I am glad that you have come.*

> Gaudeō tē vēnisse.
> *I am glad that you have come.*

580   Note: The ablative of cause (No. 781) or **propter,** *because of* (No. 992), etc., may of course also be used.

> Hāc victōriā gaudeō.
> *I rejoice at (on account of) this victory.*

---

[1]Verbs expressing joy, sorrow, surprise, anger, *etc.*, such as *gaudeō, laetor, doleō.*

CONDITIONAL SENTENCES

There are three types of conditional sentences.

581   1. NOTHING IMPLIED:

When the condition is merely stated without any implication as to the TRUTH or REALITY of the conditional clause (i. e., sī-clause).

SĪ-CLAUSE: INDICATIVE
                  TENSE BY SENSE (Nos. 521-523).

MAIN CLAUSE: Any construction that an independent clause may have (indicative; imperative; potential subjunctive; etc.).

Sī hoc vērum est, vōbīscum pācem faciam.
If this is true, I shall make peace with you.
(It is not indicated whether it is true or not.)

Sī Rōmam adieris, Tiberim vidēbis.
If you go to Rome, you will see the Tiber.
(It is not indicated whether you will go to Rome or not.)

582   2. SHOULD-WOULD:

The condition is stated as a mere *supposition* (English *should*).

BOTH CLAUSES: SUBJUNCTIVE
                  PRESENT or (RARELY) perfect without difference of meaning.

Sī veniat, eum interficiam.
Sī vēnerit, eum interfēcerim.
If he should come, I would kill him.

583 3. **CONTRARY-TO-FACT:**

The condition is stated as IMPOSSIBLE or UNTRUE.

BOTH CLAUSES: SUBJUNCTIVE

For present time, IMPER-
FECT.

For past time, PLUPER-
FECT.

Sī adesset, eum interficerem.
If he were here, I would kill him.
Were he here, I would kill him.
(It is implied that he *NOT* here NOW; present
contrary-to-fact.)

Sī adfuisset, eum interfēcissem.
If he had been present, I would have killed him.
Had he been present, I would have killed him.
(It is implied that he WAS NOT PRESENT; past
contrary-to-fact.)

Note:

584 1. **NISI,** *if . . . not, unless,* negatives the entire conditional
clause. It is particularly used when the MAIN clause
is itself NEGATIVE.

Nisi id fēceris, tē interficiam.
Unless you do this, I shall kill you.

Cīvitās cōnservārī nōn potest nisi cīvēs fortēs sunt.

A state cannot be preserved { *if the citizens are not brave.*
unless the citizens are brave.

585 2. **Sī . . . nōn,** *if . . . not,* negatives a single word in the
conditional sentence. (However, **nisi** and **sī . . . nōn**
are sometimes used without difference of meaning.)

Sī id nōn fēceris, tē interficiam.
If you do not do it, I shall kill you.

(Fēceris is emphatically negatived.)

586 3. **Sī . . . nōn** is regularly used when the MAIN clause contains **at, tamen, certē**, or some other word expressing OPPOSITION.

Virtūs, sī amīcitiam nōn gignit, certē cōnservat.

Virtue, if it does not give rise to friendship, certainly preserves it.

587 4. *But if* is **sīn** or **sīn autem:**

Hunc mihi timōrem ēripe, sī vērus est, nē opprimar, sīn falsus, ut timēre dēsinam.

Remove this fear from me; if it is well founded, that I may not be overcome, but if it is groundless, that I may cease to fear.

588 5. *But if not* is **sī minus, sīn minus, sīn aliter**, or **sī . . . nōn.**

Ēdūc etiam omnēs tuōs, sīn minus, quam plūrimōs.

Lead out also all of your followers, but if not (all), as many as possible.

589 6. *Whether . . . or* and *if . . . or if* is **sīve (seu) . . . sīve (seu).**

Sīve fēcit, sīve nōn fēcit, pūniētur.

$\left. \begin{array}{l} \textit{Whether} \\ \textit{If} \end{array} \right\}$ *he did it or not, he will be punished.*

590 7. In the main clause of a contrary-to-fact condition the indicative is regularly used with the GERUNDIVE and with the FUTURE PARTICIPLE.

Sī nōn esset cīvis, ascīscendus fuit.

If he were not a citizen, he should have been enrolled (a long time ago).

Sī advēnisset, quid fuistī factūrus?

If he had come, what would you have done?

591   8. With **possum, dēbeō, oportet,** when the possibility or obligation itself is not contrary to fact, the indicative (usually imperfect or pluperfect) is used in contrary-to-fact conditions. Otherwise these verbs follow the general rule.

> Sī voluisset, poterat mē adjuvāre.
> *If he had wished, he was able to help me.*
> (The possibility is real.)

> Nisi aegrōtārem, tē adjuvāre possem.
> *If I were not ill, I would be able to help you.*
> (The possibility is contrary to fact.)

592   9. The IMPERFECT subjunctive is sometimes used in the sī-clause of PAST contrary-to-fact conditions to express CONTINUING PAST ACTION (or state) or action contemporary with some other past action.

> Laelius, Furius, Catō, sī nihil litterīs adjuvārentur, numquam sē ad eārum studium contulissent.
>
> *Laelius, Furius, and Cato would never have devoted themselves to the study of letters, unless they had been (continuously) helped by them.*

593   10. The construction of conditional sentences may be mixed if the sense requires it.

> Sī mēns nōn laeva fuisset, Trōja nunc stāret.
> *If our mind had not been perverse, Troy would now be standing.*
> (Present and past contrary-to-fact.)

CLAUSES EXPRESSING A PROVISO OR A CONDITIONAL WISH

594　*Modo, dum, dummodo,* and *sī modo,*
'if only,' 'provided only,' 'as long as,' take the
SUBJUNCTIVE if a wish or intention is implied;
tense by sequence (Nos. 524-537);
negative: *nē.*

> Ōderint, dum metuant.
> *Let them hate, provided only they fear.*

> Magnō mē metū līberābis, modo inter mē atque tē mūrus
> intersit.
> *You will free me from a great fear, if only there be a wall
> between you and me.*

> Manēbō dummodo tū nē fugiās.
> *I shall remain provided you do not flee.*

ADVERSATIVE AND CONCESSIVE CLAUSES

595　1. *Quamquam,*[1] 'although,' generally states a FACT:
indicative; tense by sense (Nos. 521-523).

> Quamquam dīves est, beātus nōn est.
> *Although he is rich, he is not happy.*

596　2. *Cum,* 'although';
ut (negative: *nē*), 'granted that,' 'supposing that';
quamvīs, 'although,' 'however' (expressing indefinite
degree):
subjunctive; tense by sequence (Nos. 524-537).[2]

> Quamvīs dīves sīs, nōn es beātus.
> *However rich you are, you are not happy.*

----

[1] *Quamquam* is sometimes used at the beginning of a sentence to introduce a MAIN clause. It then means 'and yet.'
[2] See No. 628 for adversative clauses introduced by a relative.

Cum negāre posset, repente cōnfessus est.
Although he could have denied it, he suddenly confessed.

Ut bonus sit, sapiēns nōn est.
Granted that he is good, he is not wise.

597 3. *Licet*, 'although,' 'granted that':
subjunctive; tense by sequence (Nos. 524-537),
but it is used only in PRIMARY sequence (hence
only with the PRESENT or PERFECT).

Licet veniat, eum nōn vidēbō.

Although he $\left\{ \begin{array}{l} may \\ should \end{array} \right\}$ *come, I shall not see him.*

Licet haec dīxerim, nōn faciam.
Although I said this, I shall not do it.

598 4. *Etsī, etiamsī, tametsī*, 'even if,' 'although,' follow the
rules for conditional sentences (Nos. 581-583).

Etsī hiemēs mātūrae sunt, in Galliam proficīscī contendit.
Although the winters are early, he hastened to set out for Gaul.

Etiamsī dīves essem, beātus nōn essem.
Even if I were rich, I would not be happy.

CLAUSES OF COMPARISON

599 The indicative (tense by sense, Nos. 521-523) is regularly used in comparative clauses.

Sīc est ut dīxī.
It is (thus) as I have said.

600 But the comparative clause follows the rules for conditional sentences (Nos. 581-583) when it is the main clause of a conditional sentence with the *sī*-clause understood.

Sīc ēgit ut ego ēgissem (understood: sī adfuissem).
He acted (thus) as <u>I would have acted</u> (understood: *if I had been present*).

Note:
A comparative clause is introduced by a word indicating comparison.

601 1. In comparing VERBS: *(thus, so)* . . . *as*
(ita) . . . **quemadmodum**
(sīc) . . . **ut**
. . . **sīcut**
. . . **velut**

Sīc <u>est</u> ut <u>dīxī</u>.
It <u>is</u> (thus) as I have <u>said</u>.

602 2. In comparing ADJECTIVES or ADVERBS:
so, as . . . *as*
tam (ita) . . . **quam**

Tam <u>bona</u> est quam <u>pulchra</u>.
She is as good as she is beautiful.

603 3. In comparing indefinite SIZE:
as great, as large . . . *as*
tantus, a, um . . . **quantus, a, um**

<u>Tantum</u> est <u>quantum</u> arbitrātus sum.
It is <u>as large as</u> I thought.

604 4. In comparing indefinite KIND: *such* . . . *as*
tālis, e . . . **quālis, e**

<u>Tālis</u> est <u>quālis</u> fuit.
He is <u>such as</u> he was.

605   5. In comparing indefinite NUMBER:
> *as many . . . as*
> **tot . . . quot**
>> Tot sunt quot putāvī.
>> *There are as many as I thought.*

606   6. In comparing indefinite NUMBER OF TIMES:
> *as often . . . as*
> **totiēs . . . quotiēs** (adverbs)
>> Totiēs id fēcit quotiēs voluit.
>> *He did it as often as he wished.*

607   7. In comparing COMPARATIVE adjectives and adverbs:
> **quō . . . eō**
> **tantō . . . quantō**
>> Quō celerius (vēneris), eō melius (erit).
>> *The quicker (you come), the better (it will be).*

608   8. For *the same as* use **īdem, eadem, idem . . . quī, quae, quod.** When the verb in the second clause is not expressed, **ac (atque)** may be used instead of the relative.

> Idem sentiō quod tū dīxistī.
> *I think the same as you said.*

> Idem sentiō $\begin{Bmatrix} \text{ac} \\ \text{quod} \end{Bmatrix}$ tū.
> *I think the same as you (think).*

609   Note: **Ac** is used only before consonants; **atque** is used before both vowels and consonants.

610   9. With adverbs and adjectives (other than **īdem**; see No. 608) of likeness and difference (**perinde, aliter, alius,** etc.) use **ac (atque)** for *as* and *than.*
> Accidit perinde ac praevīderam.
> *It happened just as I foresaw.*

> Aliter accidit ac putāveram.
> *It happened otherwise than I expected.*

CONDITIONAL CLAUSES OF COMPARISON

611   Conditional clauses of comparison are introduced by:

quasi
ac sī
velut
velut sī   'as if'
ut sī   'as though'
tamquam
tamquam sī

quam sī   'than if'

subjunctive;
tense by sequence (Nos. 524-537).

Sē gerit quasi rēx <u>sit.</u>

He conducts himself { *as if* / *as though* } *he <u>were</u> king.*

Magis eum dīlēxī <u>quam sī</u> frāter meus esset.
I loved him more <u>than if</u> he were my own brother.

612   **Note:** Sometimes the imperfect or pluperfect subjunctive is
used, even though the main verb is in a primary
tense, to indicate that the statement is contrary to
fact.

Mihi loqueris quasi fūr <u>essem.</u>
You speak to me as if I <u>were</u> a thief.

SUBJUNCTIVE BY ATTRACTION

613 A subordinate clause dependent upon a subjunctive or an infinitive is attracted into the subjunctive when it does not express a fact but forms one complex idea with the governing subjunctive or infinitive.

Bonī rēgis est eōrum quibus <u>praesit</u> ūtilitātī servīre.

It is the part of a good king to serve the interests of those whom he rules.

(**Praesit** would otherwise be **praeest**.)

Nēmō avārus adhūc inventus est cui, quod <u>habēret,</u> esset satis.

No avaricious person has yet been found who was satisfied with what he had.

(**Habēret** would otherwise be **habēbat**.)

614 **Note:** When a subordinate clause forms one idea with a contrary-to-fact condition, it is attracted both into the subjunctive and into the TENSE of the governing verb.

Quid me prohibēret Epicūrēum esse, sī probārem <u>quae ille dīceret?</u>

What would prevent me from being an Epicurean, if I approved what he says?

(**Dīceret** would be **dīcit** if it were not within a contrary-to-fact condition.)

ADJECTIVE CLAUSES

RELATIVE CLAUSES

615 Relative adjective clauses are introduced by
a relative pronoun or adjective referring
to a noun or a noun-equivalent (the antecedent)
in the main clause;
indicative;
tense by sense (Nos. 521-523).[1]

> Dux quem vīdī Caesar erat.
> *The leader whom I saw was Caesar.*

Note:

616 1. The relative pronoun follows the general rule of agreement in No. 479. When the relative pronoun refers to a double antecedent it follows the rules in Nos. 475-476.

617 2. The antecedent, especially when it would be **is, ea, id** or an indefinite pronoun, is frequently omitted.

> Quī hoc dīcit errat.
> (For "Is quī hoc dīcit errat.")
> *He who says this is in error.*

618 3. The relative is never omitted.

> Vir quem vīdī Caesar erat.
> *The man I saw was Caesar.*

619 4. A relative referring to a whole clause is neuter (often with **id** in apposition to the clause).

> Sīn tū, (id) quod jam dūdum hortor, exieris . . .
> *But if you go forth, a thing which I have long been urging . . .*

---

[1]See Nos. 624-635 for special types of relative clauses that take the subjunctive. When the *sentence* expresses *repeated* action the rules given in Nos. 542-545 are to be followed.

620 5. An APPOSITIVE of the antecedent and a SUPERLA-
TIVE modifying the antecedent are regularly put in the
relative clause.

Jūra, quī mōns altus est, iter impedit.
The mountain Jura, which is high, blocks the way.

Centuriōnem quem fortissimum in castrīs habēbat mīsit.
He sent the bravest centurion he had in the camp.

621 6. The relative is sometimes attracted into the case of the
antecedent.

Hoc cōnfirmāmus illō auguriō quō dīximus.
We confirm this by the augury which we mentioned.
(By the ordinary rule **quō** would be **quod** as the object of
dīximus.)

622 7. The relative **quī, quae, quod** is frequently used in Latin
to connect a SENTENCE or a MAIN clause with the
preceding sentence or clause. It is then equivalent to
et is, is enim, or a similar expression and should be so
translated.

Quae cum ita sint, abī!
Since these things are so, depart!

(**Quae** is part of the **cum**-clause, but connects the *sentence*
with what precedes.)

. . . Quibus omnibus rēbus commōtī hostēs cōpiās trādūxērunt.
. . . *Alarmed by all these facts, the enemy led their troops
across.*

(**Quibus** is part of the *main* clause and connects it with the
preceding narration.)

623   Relative clauses may also be introduced by
relative ADVERBS, *quō,* 'whither,' *ubi,* 'where,' *quā,*
'where,' 'by what way,' *unde,* 'whence,' *etc.,* referring
to an adverb or adverbial-equivalent
expressed or implied in the main clause;
indicative;
tense by sense (Nos. 521-523).[1]

> Nāvēs <u>unde</u> profectae sunt (erant) revertērunt.
> *The ships returned (to the place) whence they had set out.*

> Locus <u>ubi</u> castra posuit tūtus erat.
> *The place where he pitched camp was safe.*

> Ex eīs regiōnibus <u>quō</u> hostēs advēnerant discessit.
> *He withdrew from those regions where the enemy had
> arrived.*

624   Relative clauses, whether introduced by relative pronouns, adjectives, or adverbs, may have the force of
other kinds of subordinate clauses:

625   PURPOSE clauses (No. 546) introduced by a relative:
subjunctive;
tense by sequence (Nos. 524-537).

> Equitēs mīsit <u>quī</u> oppidum caperent.
> *He sent cavalry to take the town.*
> *(He sent cavalry who should take the town.)*

> Locum <u>ubi</u> castra pōneret ēlēgit.
> *He selected a place to pitch camp.*
> *(He selected a place where he might pitch camp.)*

---

[1]However, when the *sentence* expresses repeated action the rules given
in Nos. 542-545 are to be followed.

626   **RESULT** clauses (No. 550) introduced by a relative:
subjunctive;
tense by sequence (Nos. 524-537, 554-555).

> Nōn is est quī hoc dīcat.
> *He is not such a one that he would say this.*
> *(He is not such as would say this.)*

627   **CAUSAL** clauses (Nos. 572-573, 578) introduced by a
relative:
subjunctive;
tense by sequence (Nos. 524-537).

> Tibi quī mē adjūverīs, grātiās agō.
> *I thank you who (because you) helped me.*

628   **ADVERSATIVE** clauses (Nos. 595-598) introduced by
a relative:
subjunctive;
tense by sequence (Nos. 524-537).

> Eum quem anteā dēfenderim, tamen amplius nōn dē-
> fendam.
> *Him whom I defended before, I shall nevertheless no
> longer defend.*
> *Although I defended him before, I shall no longer defend
> him.*

629   **CONDITIONAL clauses introduced by a relative follow the rules for conditional sentences (Nos. 581-583).**

Quī Deum esse <u>neget,</u> eum hominem esse vix putem.

I would scarcely consider him a human being who should deny that God exists.

(Equivalent to the *should-would* type: *I <u>would</u> scarcely consider him a human being if he <u>should</u> deny that God exists.*)

630   **LIMITING relative clauses introduced by *quī, quī modo, quī quidem:*
subjunctive;
tense by sequence (Nos. 524-537).**

Omnium ōrātōrum <u>quōs quidem audīverim,</u> acūtissimum jūdicō Sertorium.

Of all the orators, <u>whom at least I have heard,</u> I judge Sertorius to be the most skilled.

Note:

631   1. The relative **quod** is used in such clauses to mean *as far as.*

Epicūrus sē ūnus, <u>quod sciam,</u> sapientem profitērī ausus est.

Epicurus alone, <u>as far as I know,</u> dared to profess himself a wise man.

632   2. **Quātenus, quoad,** and **quantum,** *as far as,* always take the indicative.

Epicūrus sē ūnus, <u>quoad sciō,</u> sapientem profitērī ausus est.

Epicurus alone, as far as I know, dared to profess himself a wise man.

CHARACTERISTIC CLAUSES

633 A relative characteristic clause is used to describe the
general CHARACTER of the antecedent;
subjunctive;
tense by sequence (Nos. 524-537):

634 1. Regularly after general, indefinite, negative, and interrogative antecedents.

> Nēmō est quī hoc nesciat.
> *There is no one who does not know this.*

> Quis est quī hoc crēdat?
> *Who is there that believes this?*

635 2. Regularly after *idōneus,* 'suitable,' *aptus,* 'fit,' *dignus,*
'worthy,' *indignus,* 'unworthy,' *ūnus,* 'one,' and *sōlus,*
'only.'

> Virtūs tua digna est quae laudētur.
> *Your courage is worthy to be praised.*

> Indignī estis quibus fidem habeāmus.
> *You are not worthy of our confidence.*

636 Note: It is frequently impossible to distinguish a *characteristic clause* from a relative clause of *result* or *cause.*

NOUN CLAUSES

CLAUSES INTRODUCED BY *UT, UT NŌN, NĒ, UT NĒ*

637   Noun clauses of RESULT introduced by *ut*
(negative: *ut nōn*) and
noun clauses of PURPOSE introduced by *ut*
(negative: *nē*, sometimes *ut nē*)
take the subjunctive; tense by sequence (Nos. 524-537).

638   A noun clause of result is used as the subject of such
impersonal expressions as *accidit*, 'it happens,' *sequitur*,
'it follows,' *reliquum est*, 'it remains,' *ita fit*, 'hence it
happens,' *fierī potest*, 'it is possible,' or as the object of
faciō and its compounds, such as *efficiō*, 'bring about,'
'cause,' *cōnficiō*, 'accomplish,' *perficiō*, 'bring about.'

Accidit ut nōs nōn vidēret.
It happened that he did not see us.

Sequitur ut bonus sit.
It follows that he is good.

Effēcit ut pōns fieret.
He brought it about that a bridge was made (built).

639   A noun clause of purpose is used as the object of such
verbs as *postulō*, 'demand,' *dēcernō*, 'decree,' *persuādeō*,
'persuade,' *optō*, 'desire,' *quaerō*, 'ask,' *imperō*, 'order,'
hortor, 'urge,' *moneō*, 'advise,' *rogō*, 'ask,' *impetrō*,
'obtain.'

Persuāsit ut dē fīnibus exīrent.
He persuaded (them) to go forth from their country.

Eum monuit nē īret.
He advised him not to go.

Note:

640   1. Some verbs of this class also take the infinitive or the accusative with infinitive, especially, **volō**, *wish*, **nōlō**, *am unwilling*, **mālō**, *prefer*, **cupiō**, *desire*, **studeō**, *am eager*, **jubeō**, *command*, **licet** *(w. dative of person)*, *it is allowed*, **cōnor**, *try*, **vetō**, *forbid*, **patior**, *allow*.

> Deum vidēre cupimus.
> *We desire to see God.*

641   2. **Necesse est**, *it is necessary*, **oportet**, *it behooves*, and **licet**, *it is allowed*, take the subjunctive WITHOUT **UT**. (They may also take the infinitive, No. 892.)

> Deus sit necesse est.
> *It is necessary that God exist.*

NOUN CLAUSES AFTER VERBS OF FEARING

642   Verbs of 'fearing' take
a noun clause introduced by
nē, 'lest,' 'that'; *nē nōn* (or *ut*), 'that not';
subjunctive;
tense by sequence (Nos. 524-537).

> Timeō <u>nē</u> vincat.[1]
>
> *I fear* $\left\{ \dfrac{lest}{that} \right\}$ *he will conquer.*
>
> Timeō $\left\{ \dfrac{nē\ nōn}{\underline{ut}} \right\}$ veniat.
>
> *I fear <u>that</u> he will <u>not</u> come.*

---

[1] The subordinate clause after verbs of fearing contains a disguised wish "I fear that he will conquer" means that the writer has this wish: "May he not conquer" (*Nē vincat*, No. 511). This explains the seeming reversal of meaning in the conjunctions *nē* and *ut* in some clauses of this kind.

Note:

643   1. **Ut** must not be used for **nē nōn** when the verb of fearing is itself negative or when the negative belongs to a single word and not to the whole clause.

> Nōn vereor nē nōn veniās.
> *I do not fear that you will not come.*
> (Ut may NOT be used.)

644   *2. I fear to do* is **vereor** (**timeō**) with the infinitive as in English.

NOUN *NĒ*-CLAUSES

645   Noun clauses introduced by *nē*
take the subjunctive;
tense by sequence (Nos. 524-537).
They occur after such verbs as *caveō*, 'beware,' *vītō*, 'avoid,' *vetō*, 'forbid,' *impediō*, 'hinder,' *resistō*, 'resist,' *obstō*, 'prevent,' *dēterreō*, 'deter,' *recūsō*, 'refuse,' *prohibeō*, 'prevent.'

> Vōs prohibēbō <u>nē</u> flūmen trānseātis.
> *I shall prevent you <u>from</u> crossing the river.*

> Vōbīs obsistam <u>nē</u> flūmen trānseātis.
> *I shall oppose you <u>lest</u> you cross the river.*

> Cavē <u>nē</u> cadās.
> *Beware <u>lest</u> you fall.*

NOUN CLAUSES INTRODUCED BY *QUŌMINUS*

646   Noun clauses introduced by *quōminus*
take the subjunctive;
tense by sequence (Nos. 524-537).
They are used after verbs of 'hindering,' preventing,'
etc.

Nōn recūsāvit quōminus poenam subīret.
He did not refuse to undergo the penalty.

Quid obstat quōminus Deus sit beātus?
What prevents God from being happy?

Aetās nōn impedit quōminus litterārum studia teneāmus.
Age does not hinder our retaining interest in literature.

Note:

647   1. These verbs may also take **nē** (No. 645) and, when negative, **quīn** (No. 652).

648   2. **Nōn recūsō** may take **nē** (No. 645), **quōminus, quīn** (No. 652), or the infinitive.

       Īre nōn recūsāvit.
       He did not refuse to go.

649   3. **Prohibeō** may take **nē** (No. 645), **quōminus,** and, when negative, **quīn** (No. 652); however, oftener it takes the infinitive.

       Barbarōs intrā suōs fīnēs ingredī prohibuērunt.
       They prevented the barbarians from advancing within their (own) territory.

NOUN *QUĪN*-CLAUSES

650   Clauses introduced by *quīn* may be used ONLY when the main verb is NEGATIVE.
They take the subjunctive;
tense by sequence (Nos. 524-537).

Noun *quīn*-clauses occur:

651   1. Regularly after *nōn dubitō*, 'I do not doubt,' *dubium nōn est*, 'there is no doubt,' *nōn multum abest*, 'there is nothing wanting,' *facere nōn possum*, 'I cannot but,' *fierī nōn potest*, 'it is impossible.'

> Nōn dubitō quīn vērum sit.
> *I do not doubt that it is true.*

> Fierī nōn potest quīn veniat.
> *It is impossible that he will not come.*

652   2. Often after negative expressions, especially of 'hindering,' 'preventing,' etc.

> Hoc nōn impediet quīn vincāmus.
> *This will not keep us from conquering.*

Note:

653   1. When **quīn** is equivalent to **ut nōn,** it introduces a result clause (No. 552).

> Nihil tam difficile est quīn invēstīgārī possit.
> *Nothing is so difficult that it cannot be discovered.*

654   2. When **quīn** is equivalent to **quī nōn** or **quod nōn,** it introduces a characteristic clause (No. 634).

> Nēmō est quīn sciat.
> *There is no one who does not know.*

655 3. **Dubitāre** meaning *to doubt,* when affirmative, takes an indirect question.

> Dubitō num vērum sit.
> *I doubt whether it is true.*

656 4. **Dubitāre** meaning *to hesitate* takes the infinitive.

> Pugnāre nōn dubitāvit.
> *He did not hesitate to fight.*

NOUN *QUOD*-CLAUSES

657 *Quod,* 'the fact that' (explanatory)
takes the indicative;
tense by sense (Nos. 521-523).

These clauses may follow:

658 1. **Demonstratives, expressed or implied, in the main clause.**

> Eō (or hāc rē, eā rē, hōc) Caesar aliīs praestābat quod rēs maximās et gessit et scrīpsit.
> *In this Caesar surpassed others, that he both achieved great deeds and recorded them.*

> Quod vīvō, tuum est.
> *That I live, this I owe to you* (lit.: *is yours*).

659 2. **Expressions like** *bene (male, commodē, opportūnē) accidit (fit, ēvēnit).*

> Bene accidit quod lūna plēna erat.
> *It was fortunate that the moon was full.*

Note: For **quod** after verbs of emotion see No. 579.

INDIRECT QUESTIONS

660 **DEFINITION:** An INDIRECT question is one that depends on a verb of *saying, asking, knowing, etc.* As a noun clause it may be used as SUBJECT, OBJECT, APPOSITIVE, or PREDICATE NOUN. It is introduced by the same interrogative particles, adverbs, pronouns, and adjectives as direct questions.

661 Note: **Nōnne** is NEVER used except with **QUAERŌ.**
Num and **-ne** mean *whether (if).*
Necne is used for **annōn,** *or not,* in a double indirect question.
Quī (in this form, the nominative masculine singular *only*) is sometimes used for **quis.**

662 **INDIRECT QUESTIONS**
are put in the subjunctive;
tense by sequence (Nos. 524-537).

Caesar rogat <u>num</u> mīlitēs <u>pugnent.</u>
Caesar asks whether the soldiers are fighting.

Caesar rogat <u>num</u> mīlitēs <u>pugnāverint.</u>
Caesar asks whether the soldiers fought.

Caesar rogāvit <u>num</u> mīlitēs <u>pugnārent.</u>
Caesar asked whether the soldiers were fighting.

Caesar rogāvit <u>num</u> mīlitēs <u>pugnāvissent.</u>
Caesar asked whether the soldiers had fought.

Rogāvit quid esset factūrus.
He asked what he was going to do.

Nesciit quanta esset īnsulae magnitūdō.
He did not know how large the island was.

Sciō ubi fuerīs.
I know where you were.

Quaesīvī cognōsceretne signum.
I asked whether he recognized the seal.

Rogō utrum hoc dīxerīs necne.
I ask whether you said this or not.

INDIRECT DISCOURSE

663   **DEFINITION**: Indirect discourse is speech reported in dependence on a verb of *saying, hearing,* or the like.

    Direct: Pācem faciam.
              I shall make peace.

              "Pācem," inquit, "faciam."
              He said, "I shall make peace."

    Indirect: Dīxit sē pācem factūrum esse.
              He said he would make peace.

In indirect discourse:

664   1. **Main declarative clauses are put
       in the accusative and the infinitive;
       tense by relation (Nos. 885-887).**

       Dīxit sē ventūrum esse.
       He said that he would come.

       Crēdō eum ventūrum esse.
       I believe that he will come.

665   **2. Subordinate clauses,
            questions,
            commands (negative *nē*),
            are put in the subjunctive;
            tense by sequence (Nos. 524-537).**

Rēx lēgātīs respondit: Agrōs quōs occupāvisset[1] suōs
esse; nē in eōs Caesar exercitum dūceret.[2] Cūr Caesar
ad sē vēnisset?[3] In Prōvinciam reverterētur.[4]

*The king answered the envoys: that the fields which
he had occupied were his. Let Caesar not lead an army
into them. Why had Caesar come to him? Let him
return into the Province.*

Explanation:

1. Quōs occupāvisset is a *subordinate* clause in indirect
   discourse; therefore, the *subjunctive* is used.

2. Nē . . . dūceret is a *negative command* in indirect discourse; therefore, nē *with the subjunctive* is used.

3. Cūr . . . vēnisset is a *question* in indirect discourse;
   therefore, the *subjunctive* is used.

4. In . . . reverterētur is a *command* in indirect discourse;
   therefore, the *subjunctive* is used.

Note:

666   1. Rhetorical questions in indirect discourse are put into
            the accusative with the infinitive.

Caesar mīlitibus dīxit lēgātum ex aciē fūgisse; quid turpius
esse?

*Caesar said to the soldiers that the lieutenant had fled from
the battle line; what was more shameful?*

667 2. In indirect discourse the tense of the main verb of *saying, etc.* determines whether the tenses of the subjunctives in the indirect discourse are to be *primary* or *secondary*. But the particular tense of these subjunctives, that is, whether they are to be put in the *present* or *perfect* in primary sequence, and whether they are to be put in the *imperfect* or *pluperfect* in secondary sequence, depends upon their relation to the verb to which these subjunctives are directly subordinated.

Example and Explanation:

Dīxit sē, cum rediisset, eōs vīsūrum esse.
He said that he would see them when he returned.

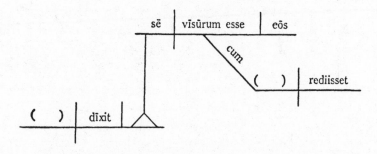

Dīxit is the verb of saying which governs the entire indirect discourse. Since then it is a *secondary* tense, the subjunctive (**rediisset**) in the indirect discourse must be a *secondary* tense. However, as the diagram shows, **rediisset** is *directly subordinated* to the infinitive **vīsūrum esse**. Now in relation to this verb, **rediisset** expresses an action *completed before* the action of **vīsūrum esse**. (The act of *returning* must be *completed before* the act of *seeing*). Therefore **rediisset** is put in the *pluperfect* and not in the imperfect.

668 3. In passing from direct to indirect discourse, pronouns and adverbs of time will change according to sense.

> **Direct:** Hodiē vēnī.
> *I came today.*
>
> **Indirect:** (Reported by a third person some days later.)
> Dīxit sē illō diē vēnisse.
> *He said he had come on that day.*

4. Conditional sentences:

669 a. The **sī**-clause is treated like any subordinate clause except that an imperfect or pluperfect subjunctive is never changed to a primary tense.

> Sciō vōs, sī possētis, mē adjūtūrōs fuisse.
> *I know that, if you were able, you would have helped me.*

b. The main clause goes into the infinitive, but:

670 1. A present subjunctive becomes a future infinitive.

> Dīcō tē, sī hoc dīcās, errātūrum esse.
> *I say that you would be in error if you should say this.*

671 2. An imperfect or pluperfect subjunctive becomes a future infinitive in **-ūrus fuisse.**

> Sciō vōs, sī potuissētis, mē adjūtūrōs fuisse.
> *I know that, if you had been able, you would have helped me.*

Note:

672 1. In the passive the imperfect or pluperfect subjunctive may change to **futūrum fuisse ut** with the imperfect subjunctive.

> Sciō, sī hoc fēcissētis, futūrum fuisse ut vituperārēminī.
> *I know that, if you had done this, you would have been blamed.*

673 2. **Posse, dēbēre, oportēre** are used as future infinitives: **potuisse, dēbuisse, oportuisse** are used as the **-ūrus fuisse** forms.

674 c. When the pluperfect subjunctive active in the main clause of a contrary-to-fact condition becomes dependent (*v. g.*, in an indirect question, an **ut-** or **quin-**clause), it is changed to the form **-ūrus fuerim** if the verb has a future participle.

> Nōn dubitō quīn, sī hoc dīxissēs, errātūrus fuerīs.
> *I do not doubt that you would have erred if you had said this.*

675 5. **Implied Indirect Discourse:** Indirect discourse is often used when a verb of *saying*, etc., is merely implied in the context.

> Rēgulus reddī captīvōs negāvit esse ūtile; illōs enim adulēscentēs esse, sē jam cōnfectum senectūte.
> *Regulus said that it would be useless to return the captives; for (he said) they were young men, he himself was already worn out with age.*
> (The context implies that the words of Regulus are being reported.)

676 6. In indirect discourse subordinate clauses which are *explanatory* or *circumlocutions* are oftener put in the INDICATIVE.

> Quis potest esse tam mente captus quī neget haec omnia quae vidēmus deōrum immortālium potestāte administrārī?
> *Who can be so stupid as to deny that all these things which we see are administered by the power of the immortal gods?*
>
> (**Haec omnia quae vidēmus** is merely a circumlocution for *all this visible world.*)

THE CASES

THE NOMINATIVE

677　The subject of a finite verb is in the nominative case.

Marīa ōrat.
Mary prays.

THE VOCATIVE

678　The person addressed is put in the vocative.

Pugnāte fortiter, mīlitēs!
Fight bravely, soldiers!

Tū, Domine, adjuvābis mē.
Thou, O Lord, wilt help me.

679　Note: In poetry and elevated prose the nominative may be used for the vocative or as an appositive to a vocative.

Audī tū, populus Albānus!
Hear you, Alban nation!

THE GENITIVE AS AN ADJECTIVE-EQUIVALENT

THE POSSESSIVE GENITIVE

680 The genitive, as attributive or predicative, is used to express the POSSESSOR.

Cōpiae hostium veniunt (attributive).
The enemy's troops are coming.

Fīlius rēgis occīsus est (attributive).
The king's son was killed.
(The son of the king was killed.)

Gallia Populī Rōmānī nōn Ariovistī est (predicative).
Gaul belongs to the Roman people not to Ariovistus.
(Gaul is the Roman People's, not Ariovistus'.)

THE EXPLANATORY GENITIVE

681 The genitive is used to EXPLAIN the noun it modifies.

The genitive may explain a noun in many ways. It may explain what an object is *made of, consists in, is connected with,* or it may simply give or limit the meaning of a noun. The exact connection and the best English translation will depend on the context.

Vōx vēritātis
The word "truth"

Perīculum mortis
Danger of death

Injūria lēgātōrum retentōrum
The wrong of (consisting in) detaining the envoys

Acervus frūmentī
A heap of grain (made of grain)

Agmen elephantōrum
A column of (made up of) elephants

Signum proeliī committendī
The signal for engaging in battle

Difficultātēs bellī
The difficulties of (connected with) the war

682 Note: Explanatory names with cities, mountains, rivers, etc., are generally not put in the *genitive* but in *apposition*.

Urbs Rōma
The city of Rome

Flūmen Arar
The river Saône

THE SUBJECTIVE GENITIVE

683 **With nouns implying an ACTION the genitive is used to express the SOURCE or DOER of that action.**

Adventus Caesaris
The arrival of Caesar
(*i. e.,* Caesar arrived.)

Injūriae Gallōrum
The wrongs of the Gauls
(*i. e.,* The Gauls *committed* the wrongs.)

THE OBJECTIVE GENITIVE

684 With nouns implying an ACTION
the genitive is used to express
the OBJECT OF THAT ACTION.

> Timor Deī
> *Fear of God*
> (*i. e.*, We fear God.)

> Caedēs prīncipum
> *The slaughter of the chiefs*
> (*i. e.*, Someone slaughtered the chiefs.)

685 Note: Notice that many English prepositional phrases are
translated by this genitive: *a remedy for anger,*
remedium īrae; *a belief in God*, opīniō Deī, *etc.*

THE PARTITIVE GENITIVE

686 The genitive is used to express the WHOLE
of which the noun it modifies expresses a part.

> Magna pars cōpiārum
> *A large part of the troops*

> Prīmus omnium mīlitum
> *First of all the soldiers*

Note:

1. The partitive genitive is used with:

687 a. nouns, neuter adjectives, neuter pronouns, of QUAN-
TITY.

> Plūs frūmentī
> *More (of) grain*

> Sī quid est in mē ingeniī
> *If there is any native talent in me*

688   b. comparatives and superlatives.

> Hōrum omnium fortissimī
> *The bravest of all these*

689   c. numerals and pronouns like **nūllus,** *no (one),* **nēmō,**
no one, **uter,** *which* (of two), etc.

> Ūnus eōrum
> *One of them*
> Nēmō eōrum
> *No one of them*

690   d. the adverbs, **satis,** *enough,* **nimis,** *too much,* **parum,**
too little, **partim,** *part of,* when used as nouns.

> Satis frūmentī
> *Enough (of) grain*

691   e. (occasionally) adverbs of place like **ubi,** *where,* **quō,**
whither, etc.

> Ubi terrārum sumus?
> *Where on earth are we?*

692   2. With numerals, comparatives, and superlatives, **ex** or **dē,**
less often **inter,** may be used to emphasize the relation
of whole and part.

> Ūnus ex multīs
> *One of many*

693   3. Only adjectives with genitives in **-ī** may be used as
nouns in the partitive genitive.

> Nihil <u>novī</u> *(genitive)*
> *Nothing new*

but:

> Nihil trīste (**trīste** *agrees* with **nihil**)
> *Nothing sad*

694   4. English often uses an *of*-phrase where there is no PART
expressed. The Latin does not use the genitive in such
cases but makes the words agree.

> *All of us* (*All* is not a PART of *us*)
> Omnēs nōs (lit.: *we all*)
>
> *All of these* (*All* is not a PART)
> Hī omnēs (lit.: *these all*)

THE DESCRIPTIVE GENITIVE

695   **The genitive, ALWAYS accompanied by an adjective,
may be used to DESCRIBE
a noun or a noun-equivalent.**

> Homō magnae virtūtis
> *A man of great courage*
>
> Fossa vīgintī pedum
> *A twenty-foot ditch* (lit.: *a ditch of twenty feet*)

Note:

1. In descriptive phrases the genitive or ablative (No. 762)
may often be used at will, but:

696   a. Phrases of size, number, weight, time, space, worth,
rank, position, value, and kind (**modus,** *sort, manner*
and **genus,** *kind*) are always in the genitive.

> Fossa vīgintī pedum
> *A twenty-foot ditch*
>
> Situs oppidī erat hūjus modī.
> *The position of the town was of this sort.*

697   b. Phrases descriptive of parts of the body or external appearances are always in the ABLATIVE.

> Puella caeruleīs oculīs
> *A blue-eyed girl*

698   c. Transient qualities or states are always in the ABLATIVE.

> Grātō animō sum.
> *I am grateful.*

699   2. The ablative and genitive of description supply in Latin for many adjectives which that language does not possess. Thus we say: *a blue-eyed girl*. But the Romans had no adjective for *blue-eyed;* hence, they said: **puella caeruleīs oculīs**, *a girl with blue eyes*.

THE GENITIVE AS AN ADVERB-EQUIVALENT

THE GENITIVE OF INDEFINITE VALUE

700 The genitive neuter singular of adjectives of quantity is used with verbs of 'estimating,' 'valuing,' and the like to express INDEFINITE value.

> Est tantī!
> *It is worth it! (It is of such a value.)*

> Permagnī eum aestimō.
> *I value him very highly.*

Note:

701   1. The common genitives in this case are:

magnī	*of great value, highly*
permagnī	*of very great value, very highly*
plūris	*of higher value, more (highly)*
plūrimī } maximī }	*of highest value, very highly (highest)*
parvī	*of small value, very little*
minōris	*of less value, less highly*
minimī	*of smallest value, very little*
tantī	*of such a value, so much*
quantī	*of what value, how highly*

702   2. The common verbs in this case are:

aestimō,	*1, tr.*	*value, estimate*
faciō,	*3, tr.*	*regard*
habeō,	*2, tr.*	*hold*
dūcō,	*3, tr.*	*consider*
putō,	*1, tr.*	*think*
sum,	*intr.*	*am*

703   3. The genitives **nihilī** *(nothing)*, **floccī** *(a straw)*, and **assis** *(a cent)*, and a few similar words may also be used in this construction, the last two generally after a negative.

> Nōn habeō eum assis.
> *I don't consider him worth a cent.*

704   4. Adverbs are more rarely used with these verbs than the genitive.

> Eum parvē aestimō.
> *I value him little.*

705   5. The genitives **tantī, quantī, plūris, minōris,** are used as genitives of price with verbs of *buying, selling, costing,* and the like instead of the ablative of price (No. 788). Otherwise the ablative of price is used with such verbs.

> Quantī stat?
> *How much does it cost?*

THE GENITIVE WITH VERBS

706   After *meminisse* and *oblīvīscī:*
persons are put in the genitive;
things in the accusative or genitive
(but neuter pronouns or adjectives are always in the accusative).

> Mementō meī.
> *Remember me.*

> Oblīvīscere incendiōrum!
> *Forget burnings!*

> Hoc meminī.
> *I remember this.*

Note:

707   1. **Meminisse,** however, takes the accusative of persons when it means not merely *remember,* but *still remember one known personally.*

>   Caesarem meminit.
>   *He remembers Caesar.*

708   2. **Recordor,** *1, tr., recall,* takes **dē** and the ablative of PERSONS but the accusative, rarely **dē** with the ablative, of THINGS.

>   Haec recordor.
>   *I recall these things.*
>
>   Dē amīcīs recordātus sum.
>   *I recalled (the thought of) my friends.*

709   With *interest* and *refert:*[1]
the person interested is put in the genitive.

>   Hoc <u>Caesaris</u> interest.
>   *This is of interest to <u>Caesar</u>.*

Note:

710   1. When the person is expressed by a pronoun the ABLATIVE FEMININE SINGULAR of the POSSESSIVE adjective is used instead of the genitive of the personal pronoun. Thus: **meā, tuā, šuā, nostrā, vestrā,** are used instead of **meī, tuī, suī, nostrī, vestrī.**

>   <u>Meā</u> refert. (*not:* <u>Meī</u> refert.)
>   *It concerns me.*

---

[1]Both these verbs are used IMPERSONALLY (No. 331). *Interest* means 'it interests,' 'it is important,' 'it makes a difference.' *Refert* means 'it concerns,' 'it matters,' 'it profits.'

711   2. The thing in question may be expressed by a neuter pronoun, an infinitive, an accusative with the infinitive, an indirect question, or a noun clause of purpose.

> Omnium interest <u>valēre.</u>
> *Good health is the concern of everyone.*

712   3. The purpose with reference to which the thing is of interest or value goes into the accusative with **ad.**

> <u>Ad discendum</u> magnī interest.
> *It is of great importance for learning.*

713   4. The degree of value or interest is expressed by an adverb, an adverbial neuter, or by the indefinite genitive of value.

> Ad discendum <u>magnī (multum)</u> interest.
> *It is of great importance for learning.*

714   With *piget, pudet, paenitet, taedet, miseret:*
the PERSON feeling the emotion is put in the ACCUSATIVE;
the CAUSE OF THE EMOTION in the GENITIVE.

> Taedet <u>mē vītae.</u>
> *I am weary of life.*
>
> Mē tuī pudet.
> *I am ashamed of you.*

715   **Note:**   piget, pigēre, piguit, **2, tr.,** *it annoys*
           paenitet, paenitēre, paenituit, **2, tr.,** *it repents*
           miseret, miserēre, miseritum est, **2, tr.,** *it grieves*
           pudet, pudēre, puduit, **2, tr.,** *it shames*
           taedet, taedēre, taeduit (taesum est), **2, tr.,** *it wearies*

716 All these verbs are used *impersonally*. However, they may have an *infinitive* or a neuter pronoun (singular or plural) as a subject.

> Haec tē pudent.
> *These things shame you.*

THE GENITIVE OF THE CHARGE

717 The genitive is used
with verbs of 'accusing,' 'condemning,' and 'acquitting' to express the CHARGE.

> Fūrtī mē accūsat.
> *He accuses me of theft.*

> Inertiae nēquitiaeque mē condemnō.
> *I condemn myself for criminal negligence.*

718 Note: **Dē** and **propter** are sometimes used. Note the phrases **dē vī,** *of assault,* and **inter sīcāriōs,** *of murder* (lit.: *among murders*).

OTHER VERBS GOVERNING THE GENITIVE

719 1. *Admoneō, admonēre, admonuī, admonitus,* 2, tr., 'warn,' 'advise'; *commoneō, etc.,* 'remind'; *commonefaciō, commonefacere, commonefēcī, commonefactus,* 3, tr., 'remind,' 'admonish,'
besides taking an accusative of the PERSON sometimes take a genitive of the THING (but always the accusative of neuter nouns and adjectives). They rarely take *dē* with the ablative of the thing.

> Hūjus reī tē commonefaciō.
> *I admonish you of this thing.*

> Tē hoc moneō.
> *I warn you of this.*

720 2. **Verbs meaning 'want,' 'need,' and 'fill with'
take either the genitive or the ablative.**

> Armōrum indigēmus.
> *We need arms.*

> Mūrum hominibus complēvit.
> *He filled the wall with men.*

721 3. *Potior, potīrī, potītus sum,* 4, intr., 'gain possession of,'
regularly takes the ablative
but occasionally takes the genitive (always the genitive in the phrase *rērum potīrī,* 'to get control of affairs').

> Castrīs potītus est.
> *He gained possession of the camp.*

GENITIVE WITH ADJECTIVES

722 **Adjectives meaning 'full,' 'possessing,' 'knowing,'
'desiring,' etc., and their contraries
often take the genitive.**

> Hūjus reī perītus
> *Skilled in this matter*

> Bellum est perīculōrum plēnum.
> *War is full of dangers.*

> Caesar glōriae cupidus erat.
> *Caesar was desirous of glory.*
> *Caesar was eager for glory.*

Note:

723   1. Common adjectives with the genitive are:

plēnus, a, um, *full* (occasionally also with the ablative); inānis, e, *empty of;* indigēns, indigentis, *lacking;* particeps, *sharing in;* proprius, a, um, *proper to;* commūnis, e, *common to;* perītus, a, um, *skilled in;* memor, *mindful of;* imperītus, a, um, *unskilled in;* cupidus, a, um, *eager for;* studiōsus, a, um, *eager for, zealous for.* Similis, e, *like,* generally takes the dative, but the genitive is more common with persons and stresses the exactness of the likeness.

724   2. Present participles expressing not a single action but an habitual quality or a continuous state may govern the genitive.

Amāns patriae
A lover of his country (i. e., a patriot)

THE DATIVE

THE DATIVE OF POSSESSION

725   The dative is used with *esse*
to express the possessor.

> Pater mihi est.
> *I have a father (a father is to me).*

> Domus tibi est.
> *You have a house (a house is to you).*

THE DATIVE OF REFERENCE

726   The dative is used to express the person
(or, more rarely, the thing)
TO WHOM a statement refers or is of interest,
or FOR WHOM it is true.

> Nōn nōbīs sōlīs sed et patriae nātī sumus.
> *We are born, not for ourselves alone, but also for our country.*

> Ille mihi semper deus erit.
> *He will always be a god to me.*

> Hoc est oppidum prīmum Thessaliae venientibus ab Ēpīrō.
> *This is the first town of Thessaly to those coming from Epirus.*

Note:

727 1. This dative often expresses personal interest or emotion (*ethical dative*). Especially are the datives **mihi, tibi, vōbīs, nōbīs** so used.

> Quid <u>mihi</u> Celsus agit?
> *And how is <u>my</u> Celsus doing?*

728 2. In the expression **nōmen est,** the name is sometimes attracted into the dative but more often it is in the nominative in apposition with **nōmen.**

> Mihi Caesarī nōmen est.
> Mihi Caesar nōmen est.
> *My name is Caesar.*

THE DATIVE OF PURPOSE

729 The dative of an abstract noun is often used to express the purpose or tendency of an action,
especially after verbs of 'motion,' *esse,* and *relinquō.*

> Labiēnum <u>subsidiō</u> mittit.
> *He sends Labienus to help.*

> Decem cohortēs <u>auxiliō</u> mīsit.
> *He sent ten cohorts to help (for a help).*

> Duās legiōnēs <u>praesidiō</u> relīquit.
> *He left two legions behind as a garrison.*

730 **Note:**

1. The dative of purpose is never plural.
2. It is never modified by a genitive.
3. It is never modified by any adjective except one of quantity.

THE DOUBLE DATIVE

731   The dative of purpose is generally accompanied
by a dative of reference,
especially after *esse*.

> Hoc mihi magnō dolōrī est.
> *This is a great sorrow to me.*

> Suīs labōrantibus Labiēnum subsidiō mittit.
> *He sends Labienus to help his struggling men (as a help to his struggling men).*

DATIVE OF AGENCY

The dative is used to express the agent:

732   1. With the gerundive and *esse*
(except when there is another dative in the same
clause, No. 882).

> Rōmānī nōbīs vincendī sunt.
> *The Romans must be conquered by us.*

> Caesar sibi nōn exspectandum esse putāvit.
> *Caesar thought that he ought not to wait.*

733   2. More rarely with the perfect passive participle,
alone or in the compound tenses.

> Illud mihi intellectum est.
> *I understood that.*
> (Lit.: *That was understood by me.*)

734   3. Rarely with other passive forms.

> Neque cernitur ūllī.
> *And is not seen by anyone.*

THE DATIVE OF LIMIT OF MOTION

735 The dative is used in poetry to express the 'place to' or 'towards which.'

> It clāmor caelō.
> *A shout goes up to the sky.*

THE DATIVE OF THE INDIRECT OBJECT

736 DEFINITION: The INDIRECT OBJECT states the person (rarely the thing) to whom something is said, given, handed over, etc.

737 The indirect object is put in the dative.

> Gallīs gladiōs dedit.
> *He gave swords to the Gauls.*
> *He gave the Gauls swords.*

THE DATIVE AFTER COMPOUND VERBS

738 Many verbs compounded with the prepositions *ad, ante, circum, cum, in, inter, ob, post, prae, prō, sub, super* take a dative as well as an accusative object.

> Mūnītiōnī Labiēnum praefēcit.
> *He put Labienus in charge of the fortifications.*

THE DATIVE AFTER INTRANSITIVE VERBS

739   Many intransitive verbs take a sole object in the dative.

Ventus <u>nāvibus</u> nocuit.
The wind injured the <u>ships</u>.

Note:

740   1. Some of the common verbs which take this construction
       are:

> prōsum, prōdesse, prōfuī, prōfutūrus, *intr. (dat.), profit,
> benefit*
>
> noceō, nocēre, nocuī, nocitūrus, *2, intr. (dat.), injure,
> harm*
>
> studeō, studēre, studuī, *2, intr. (dat.), be eager for, devote
> energy to*
>
> cēdō, cēdere, cessī, cessūrus, *3, intr. (dat.), yield*
>
> resistō, resistere, restitī, *3, intr. (dat.), resist*
>
> parcō, parcere, pepercī, parsūrus, *3, intr. (dat.), spare*
>
> placeō, placēre, placuī, placitum, *2, intr. (dat.), please*
>
> displiceō, displicēre, displicuī, displicitum, *2, intr. (dat.),
> displease*
>
> imperō, *1, intr. (dat.), order, enjoin*
>
> persuādeō, persuādēre, persuāsī, persuāsum, *2, intr.
> (dat.), persuade*
>
> serviō, *4, intr. (dat.), serve*

741   2. Intransitive verbs are used only IMPERSONALLY in
       the passive (No. 332). The agent is in the ablative after
       ab (ā); the dative remains.

> Active: *Caesar persuades me.*
>   Caesar mihi persuādet.
>
> Passive: *I am persuaded by Caesar.*
>   Mihi ā Caesare persuādētur.
>   (Lit.: *It is persuaded to me by Caesar.*)

DATIVE WITH ADJECTIVES

The dative is used with many adjectives:

742 1. Meaning 'friendly,' 'unfriendly,' 'similar,' 'dissimilar,' 'equal,' 'unequal,' 'near,' 'related to,' and the like.

> <u>Mihi</u> amīcus est.
> *He is friendly to me.*

> Proximī sunt <u>Germānīs</u>.
> *They are next to the Germans.*

743 2. Meaning 'suitable,' 'adapted,' 'fit.'

> <u>Castrīs</u> idōneus locus
> *A place suitable for a camp*

DATIVE WITH VERBS OF SEPARATION

744 Some verbs of 'taking away,' especially those compounded with *ab (ā)*, *dē*, and *ex (ē)*, take a dative of the person.

> Hunc <u>mihi</u> timōrem ēripe.
> *Take this fear <u>from me</u>.*

THE ACCUSATIVE AS PART OF THE PREDICATE

THE ACCUSATIVE AS OBJECT

745 The direct object of a transitive verb is in the accusative.

> Caesar fortūnam laudāvit.
> *Caesar praised fortune.*

> Ūnam partem Belgae incolunt.
> *The Belgians inhabit one part.*

THE DOUBLE ACCUSATIVE

746 Verbs of 'calling,' 'electing,' 'considering as,' 'showing oneself,'
take an accusative object
and a predicate accusative (noun or adjective).

> Tē imperātōrem appellō.
> *I call you emperor.*

> Mē sevērum praebeō.
> *I show myself unrelenting.*

747 Note: In the passive:

1. the accusative object becomes the *subject;*
2. the predicate accusative becomes the *predicate nominative.*

> Active: Chrīstum rēgem appellāmus.
> *We call Christ king.*

> Passive: Chrīstus ā nōbīs rēx appellātur.
> *Christ is called king by us.*

748 *Trānsportāre, trādūcere, trājicere,* **and the like**
take two accusatives:
one of the thing transported; the other of the place.

> Caesar exercitum flūmen trādūxit.
> *Caesar led his army across the river.*

Note:

749 1. In the passive:
the thing transported becomes the *subject;*
the other accusative *remains.*

> Exercitus ā Caesare flūmen trāductus est.
> *The army was led across the river by Caesar.*

750 2. The place may also be expressed by **trāns** and the accusative.

> Helvētiī cōpiās suās trāns flūmen trādūxerant.
> *The Helvetians had led their troops across the river* (active).

> Cōpiae trāns flūmen ab Helvētiīs erant trāductae.
> *The troops had been transported across the river by the Helvetians* (passive).

751 **Verbs of 'teaching,' 'requesting,' 'demanding,' 'asking,'**
'inquiring,' and *cēlō,* 'conceal,'
take two accusatives:
one of the PERSON, the other of the THING.

> Chrīstus nōs viam salūtis docet.
> *Christ teaches us the way of salvation.*

> Rem Caesarem cēlāvit.
> *He concealed the affair from Caesar.*

> Helvētiōs frūmentum flāgitāvit.
> *He demanded grain from the Helvetians.*

Note:

752 1. Quaerō, *inquire,* always, and other verbs of *asking* and *inquiring* generally, take **ex** (**ē**) or **ab** (**ā**) with the ablative of the PERSON. Preferred usage must be learned from the dictionary. When the THING is expressed by a neuter pronoun, the double accusative is common.

> Ex tē causam bellī quaerō.
> *I ask you the cause of the war.*
>
> Hoc tē rogō.
> *I ask this of you.*

753 2. In the PASSIVE:

a. the *person* becomes the *subject;*

b. the *thing* remains *accusative.*

> **Active:** Mē linguam Latīnam docuit.
> *He taught me Latin.*
>
> **Passive:** Linguam Latīnam doctus sum.
> *I have been taught Latin.*

754 3. Many of these verbs are rare in the passive. Occasionally the THING becomes the subject.

> Frūmentum ab eīs flāgitābātur.
> *Grain was being demanded from them.*

ACCUSATIVE OF NEUTER PRONOUNS AND ADJECTIVES

An accusative of a neuter pronoun or adjective (especially of NUMBER or QUANTITY) is often used:

755 1. As an object of many INTRANSITIVE DATIVE verbs.

> Hoc Caesarī persuāsit. (**Hoc** is accusative.)
> *He persuaded Caesar of this.*

756   **2. As an object of many INTRANSITIVE verbs.**

Multa peccat.
He makes many mistakes.
(Lit.: *He errs many things.*)

Hoc gaudeō. (**Hoc** is accusative.)
I rejoice at this.

757   **3. As a SECOND object of TRANSITIVE verbs.**

Illud tē moneō.
I warn you of that.

THE COGNATE ACCUSATIVE

758   An accusative of a word of the same stem or meaning
as the verb,
generally accompanied by an adjective or pronoun,
may be used as the object
even of an otherwise intransitive verb.

Vītam jūcundam vīvere
To live a happy life

Ācerrimam pugnam pugnāre
To fight a bitter battle

THE ACCUSATIVE AS AN ADVERB-EQUIVALENT

THE ACCUSATIVE IN EXCLAMATIONS

759 The accusative is used in exclamations.

> Mē miserum!
> *Wretch that I am! (Wretched me!)*

THE ACCUSATIVE OF SPECIFICATION

760 In poetry the accusative is used to express the part affected.

> Lacrimīs oculōs suffūsa nitentēs
> *With her shining eyes filled with tears*
> (Lit.: *Filled with tears as to her shining eyes*)

THE ACCUSATIVE OF EXTENT OF SPACE AND TIME

761 The accusative is used to express the extent of space or time (answering the questions: How far? How long?).

> Duās hōrās pugnāvērunt.
> *They fought* $\begin{cases} \textit{two hours.} \\ \textit{for two hours.} \end{cases}$

> Duo mīlia passuum iter fēcērunt.
> *They marched two miles.*

> Flūmen decem pedēs aberat.
> *The river was ten feet away.*

THE ABLATIVE AS AN ADJECTIVE-EQUIVALENT

THE ABLATIVE OF DESCRIPTION

762   The ablative, always accompanied by an adjective,
       may be used, attributively or predicatively,
       to describe a noun or noun-equivalent.

> Caesar erat vir summō ingeniō.
> *Caesar was a man of the highest genius.*

> Puer caeruleīs oculīs
> *A blue-eyed boy*
> *A boy with blue eyes*

> Vir magnō corpore
> *A man with a large body*

763   Note: For the distinction between the ablative of descrip-
       tion and the genitive of description see Nos. 696-699.

THE ABLATIVE AS AN ADVERB-EQUIVALENT

THE ABLATIVE OF THE AGENT

764   *Ā* or *ab* with the ablative is used to express
       the LIVING AGENT.

> Deus ā Chrīstiānīs laudātur.
> *God is praised by Christians.*

> Urbs ā duce oppugnāta est.
> *The city was attacked by the leader.*

> Hostēs ab eīs pulsī sunt.
> *The enemy were routed by them.*

THE ABLATIVE OF MEANS

765   The ablative without a preposition is used to express the non-living agent, the means, or the instrument.

Rōmānī *tēlīs* hīberna dēfendērunt.
The Romans defended the winter quarters <u>with darts</u>.

Castra *fossā* mūnīvērunt.

They fortified the camp $\left\{\begin{array}{l} with \\ by\ means\ of \end{array}\right\}$ <u>*a ditch.*</u>

<u>Montibus</u> continēbantur.
They were held in <u>by mountains</u>.

<u>Tēlīs</u> terrentur.
They are being terrified <u>by darts</u>.

THE ABLATIVE OF SEPARATION

766   With verbs and adjectives of 'separating,' 'freeing,' 'depriving,' and the like:

1. With things: use the ablative without a preposition.
2. With persons: use the ablative with *dē, ex,* or *ab.*

Metū līber sum.
I am free from fear.

Ā tyrannīs patriam līberāvī.
I freed my country from tyrants.

Note:

767   1. Many verbs, however, require a preposition with both persons and things. Such verbs must be learned individually from the vocabularies.

768 2. With **nāscor, nāscī, nātus sum, *3, intr.,* am born,** and **orior, orīrī, ortus sum, *4, intr.,* arise, spring from,** the ablative without a preposition is generally used to express *immediate source,* but **ab (ā)** or **ex (ē)** with the ablative to express *remote source.*

> Nāte deā!
> *Goddess-born!* (immediate source).

> Ā Germānīs ortī sunt.
> *They are descended from the Germans* (remote source).

THE ABLATIVE OF MANNER

769 *Cum* **with the ablative is used to express manner and attendant circumstances. When the noun is modified by an adjective** *cum* **may be omitted.**

> Mīlitēs cum virtūte pugnāvērunt.
> *The soldiers fought with courage.*

> Mīlitēs magnā (cum) virtūte pugnāvērunt.
> *The soldiers fought with great courage.*

THE ABLATIVE OF RESPECT

770 **The ablative without a preposition is used to express respect (answering: In what? In respect to what?).**

> Lēgibus inter sē differunt.
> *They differ among themselves in laws.*

> Aliōs virtūte superant.
> *They surpass others* $\begin{cases} \textit{in courage.} \\ \textit{in respect to courage.} \\ \textit{with regard to courage.} \end{cases}$

THE ABLATIVE OF DEGREE OF DIFFERENCE

771 The ablative is used to express the degree of difference with comparatives and comparative expressions.

Multō melior est.
He is much better (lit.: *by much*).

THE ABLATIVE OF ACCOMPANIMENT

772 *Cum* with the ablative is used to express accompaniment or association.

Lēgātus cum Caesare vēnit.

The envoy came { *in company with* / *together with* / *with* } *Caesar.*

Ūnā cum eīs proficīscuntur.
They set out with them.

Germānī sēsē cum hīs conjūnxērunt.
The Germans united themselves with these.
(i. e., *the Germans joined these.*)

773 Note: In military expressions **cum** is sometimes omitted when the noun is modified by an adjective other than a numeral.

Omnibus cōpiīs subsequitur.
He follows with all his forces.
He follows in full force.

774 This is especially the case when, e. g., an army is considered rather as the means.

Exercitū urbem cēpit.
He took the city with his army.
(He took the city by means of his army.)

THE ABLATIVE WITH ADJECTIVES

775 The ablative is used with adjectives meaning 'worthy of,' 'full of,' 'relying on,' and the like.

Vir laude dignus
A man worthy of praise

776 Note: Such adjectives are especially **dignus, a, um,** *worthy of;* **indignus, a, um,** *unworthy of;* **plēnus, a, um,** *full of* (which generally takes the genitive, see No. 722); **frētus, a, um,** *relying on;* **contentus, a, um,** *contented with,* etc.

THE ABLATIVE OF COMPARISON

777 When *quam,* 'than,' would be followed
by the nominative or the accusative,
the ablative may be substituted
for *quam* and the nominative or accusative.

Patria mihi vītā cārior est (*i. e.,* quam vīta).
My country is dearer to me than life.

Note:

778 1. The ablative is always used instead of **quam** and the nominative or accusative of the RELATIVE pronoun.

Patria, quā nihil mihi cārius est, mēcum loquitur.
My country, than which nothing is dearer to me, speaks with me.

779 2. The ablative is never used when it would be ambiguous.

I love Cicero more than Brutus (does).
Cicerōnem plūs amō quam Brūtus.
(Brūtō would substitute for either Brūtus or Brūtum; therefore it is not used.)

780   3. The ablative is regular in negative and interrogative sentences.

> Nihil eō dulcius.
> *Nothing is more pleasant than that.*
> *Nobody is more delightful than he.*

THE ABLATIVE OF CAUSE

781   **The ablative is sometimes used to express the cause or reason.**

> Victōriā gaudet.
> *He rejoices in his victory (because of his victory, on account of his victory).*

> Spē dēlector.
> *I take delight in hope.*

Note:

782   1. This is especially common with verbs of emotion like **gaudeō,** *rejoice;* **laetor,** *rejoice;* etc.

783   2. Cause is more often expressed by prepositions, such as **propter, ob,** *on account of,* with the accusative.

784   3. The *preventing cause* is expressed by **prae** and the ablative.

> Prae gaudiō loquī nōn potuit.
> *He was unable to speak for joy.*

THE ABLATIVE AS OBJECT

785   The object of *ūtor, fruor, fungor, potior, vescor,* and their compounds is put in the ablative.

> Eōdem cōnsiliō ūsī sunt.
> *They used the same plan.*

Note:

786   1. For **potior** with the genitive see No. **721.**

787   2. ūtor, ūtī, ūsus sum, *3, intr., use*
     fruor, fruī, frūctus sum, *3, intr., enjoy*
     fungor, fungī, fūnctus sum, *3, intr., perform*
     potior, potīrī, potītus sum, *4, intr., gain possession of*
     vescor, vescī, *3, intr., feed on*

THE ABLATIVE OF PRICE

788   The ablative of a noun,
of a noun and an adjective,
or of a neuter adjective of quantity
is used with verbs of 'buying,' 'selling,' 'costing,' *etc.,*
to express the PRICE.

> Domum vīlī pretiō vēndidit.
> *He sold the house cheap (for a small price).*

> Corpus aurō vēndidit.
> *He sold the body for gold.*

789   **Note:** But the genitives **tantī, quantī, plūris, minōris,** are used with these verbs instead of the ablative (see No. 705).

> Quantī cōnstat?
> *What does it cost?*
> *How much does it cost?*

PRONOUNS

DEMONSTRATIVE PRONOUNS

790 DEFINITION: A demonstrative is a word that POINTS OUT.

This book ; *that* sword ; *these ; those* men.

791
The demonstratives are:

hic, haec, hoc, 'this' (pl. 'these')
is, ea, id, 'that' (pl. 'those')
ille, illa, illud, 'that' (pl. 'those')
iste, ista, istud, 'that' (pl. 'those')

792 *Hic* points out that which is close to the speaker.
Is is unemphatic and points to the person or thing spoken of.
Ille points to that which is distant or emphasized.
Iste points out that which is near the person spoken to.

1. *Hic, is, ille, iste,* may be used:

793   a. as PRONOUNS (rule of agreement, No. 479).

> Caesar rēgem hostium cēpit. Hunc occīdit.
> *Caesar captured the king of the enemy. This man he killed.*

> Illa vēra erant.
> *Those things were true.*

794   b. as ADJECTIVES (rules of agreement, Nos. 477-478).

> Hanc urbem cēpērunt.
> *They captured this city.*

In eōs mīlitēs impetum fēcit.
He made an attack on those soldiers.

795 2. When *hic* and *ille* are used in CONTRAST,
hic refers to the thing that is closer
or that has been mentioned more recently ('the latter');
ille refers to the thing that is farther away
or that has been mentioned previously ('the former').

Hanc urbem jam habēmus; illam urbem oppugnā-
bimus.
*We already have this city; that city (yonder) we
shall attack.*

796 3. *Is* is regularly used as the personal pronoun of the
THIRD person. Less frequently *ille* is so used. *Ille*
is always more emphatic.

Caesar eum occīdit.
Caesar killed him.

Ille captus erat.
He had been captured.

797 4. *Is* (less frequently *ille*) is used as the antecedent of
the relative.

Is quī sine spē pugnat, nōn fortiter pugnat.
He who fights without hope, does not fight bravely.

798 5. *Ille*, especially when it follows the noun it modifies,
often means 'the famous.'

Caesar ille
The famous Caesar

799 6. *Iste* often implies contempt. (*Iste* therefore translates the English 'that' when spoken in scorn.)

> Iste homō!
> *That fellow!*

REFLEXIVE PRONOUNS

800 *Ego (nōs), tū (vōs)*, with the adjectives *meus, a, um,
noster, nostra, nostrum, tuus, a, um, vester, vestra, vestrum*, are also used as REFLEXIVES of the first and
second persons for 'myself,' 'ourselves,' 'yourself,' 'your-
selves,' 'my own,' 'your own,' etc.

> Patrem tuum occīdistī.
> *You killed your own father.*

801 The reflexive pronoun of the third person is:

> suī (sibi, sē, sē), *him, himself, her, herself, it, itself,
> them, themselves, oneself.*

802 The reflexive possessive of the third person is:

> suus, a, um, *his, his own, her, her own, its, its own, their,
> their own, one's, one's own.*

Suī and *suus* MUST BE USED rather than forms of
is (or *ille*):

> (Direct Reflexive)

803 1. When a pronoun of the THIRD person
refers to the subject of its OWN CLAUSE.

> Sē rēx laudāvit.
>
> *The king praised himself.*
>
> Sē interfēcit.
>
> *He killed himself.*

(Indirect Reflexive)

804   2. When a pronoun of the third person
in an accusative with the infinitive,
in a purpose clause,
or in an indirect question
refers to the subject of the MAIN clause.

Dīxit suōs ventūrōs esse.

He said his (own) men would come.

Caesar dīxit sē pugnātūrum esse.

Caesar said that he would fight.

805   3. When a pronoun of the third person
in a subjunctive clause which expresses the thought,
intention, or will of the agent of the action
in the MAIN clause
refers to the subject of the MAIN clause.

Caesar mīlitibus imperāvit ut sē sequerentur.

Caesar ordered the soldiers to follow him.

Mīlitēs laudāvit quod sē dēfendissent.

He praised the soldiers because they had defended him.

Dīxit eōs quī sē dēfendissent praemia acceptūrōs esse.

*He said that those who defended him would receive
rewards.*

Note:

806 1. Otherwise the forms of the non-reflexives **is, ea, id** (**ille, illa, illud** and **ējus, eōrum, illōrum, illīus**) must be used for the pronoun of the third person.

807 2. The reflexive forms are sometimes used to refer to other cases than that of the subject.

> Hannibalem suī cīvēs ē cīvitāte ējēcērunt.
> *His own fellow citizens expelled Hannibal from the state.*

THE INTENSIVE PRONOUN

808 1. *Ipse, ipsa, ipsum,* is frequently used as an adjective to strengthen nouns and personal pronouns (expressed or implied). It is to be translated as 'himself,' 'herself,' 'itself,' 'themselves.' The MEANING of the word which *ipse* modifies or refers to determines which of the translations of *ipse* is to be used.

> Caesar ipse vēnit.
> *Caesar himself came.*
> (Caesar is a man; therefore: *himself.*)

> Ipsa vēritās pulchra est.
> *Truth itself is beautiful.*
> (Truth is a thing; therefore: *itself.*)

> Ipsī vēnērunt.
> *They themselves came.*
> (**Ipsī** agrees with the subject of **vēnērunt**, *they*; therefore: *themselves.*)

809   2. *Ipse, ipsa, ipsum,* especially when used with a demon-
        strative pronoun *(hic, is, ille, iste),* may sometimes
        be translated by the adjective 'very.'

        In hāc ipsā urbe
        In this very city

810   3. *Ipse* is often used to strengthen REFLEXIVE pro-
        nouns. In this case however *ipse* often agrees not
        with the reflexive pronoun but with the subject of
        the clause.

        Rēx sē ipse laudat.
        The king praises himself. (**Ipse** strengthens **sē** but
        agrees with **rēx** in the nominative.)

811   4. *Ipse* may be used to strengthen a POSSESSIVE ad-
        jective. It is then put in the GENITIVE as though
        the adjective were a possessive genitive.

        Propter nostram ipsōrum salūtem fūgimus.
        We fled on account of our own safety.

        Tuum ipsīus patrem nōn dēfendistī.
        You did not defend your own father.

812   5. *Ipse* may also be used as a pronoun. It is then trans-
        lated as a pronoun of the third person with or with-
        out 'himself,' 'herself,' *etc.*

        Caesar servōs rēgis occīdit. Ipsum cēpit.
        *Caesar killed the servants of the king. Him (the king
        himself) he took captive.*

        Caesar lēgātōs dīmīsit. Ipse ad flūmen contendit.
        *Caesar dismissed the envoys. He (himself) hastened to
        the river.*

ĪDEM, EADEM, IDEM

813 *Idem, eadem, idem,* 'same,' may be used either as an adjective or as a pronoun.

Adjective: In eōdem locō castra posuit.
He pitched camp in the same place.

Pronoun: Eadem dīxit.
He said the same things.

814 *Idem* in apposition with a subject or object often has the force of 'also,' 'likewise.'

Quod idem mihi accidit.
Which also happened to me (lit.: *which same thing*).

Bonus vir quem eundem sapientem appellāmus.
A good man whom we also call wise.

SOME

Someone (somebody), something, some:

1. Opposed to 'no one,' 'none':

815 a. Pronoun: **aliquis, aliquid,** *someone, something.*
Adjective: **aliquis, aliqua, aliquod,** *some.*

Aliquem vīdī.
I saw somebody.

Ad mē aliquōs librōs mitte.
Send me some books.

816   b. **Nōnnūllī, ae, a,** *some, a few,* or
           sunt quī, *there are (those) who* . . .
           and a characteristic clause (No. 633).

   Nōnnūllī dē nostrō interitū cōgitant.
   Some meditate our destruction.

   Sunt quī dē nostrō interitū cōgitent.
   Some meditate our destruction.
   [Lit.: *There are (those) who meditate our destruction.*]

817   2. **'Some' in the sense of 'considerable number':**
           aliquot **(indeclinable adjective), 'some.'**

   Jam aliquot annōs
   Now for some years

   3. **'Someone' ('some') in the sense of 'someone (some)**
   or other':

818   a. Pronoun: **quispiam, quidpiam (or quippiam),**
                       someone, something.

   Adjective: **quispiam, quaepiam, quodpiam,** *some.*

   Quaeret quispiam.
   Somebody or other will ask.

819   b. Pronoun: **nesciōquis, nesciōquid,**
                       someone, something.

   Adjective: **nesciōquī, nesciōqua, nesciōquod,**
                       some.

   Nesciōquis vēnit.
   Someone or other came.

820 **4.** 'Someone' ('some'), 'a certain' in the sense of 'a certain one,' 'some definite one' (equivalent to the English indefinite article):

Pronoun: **quīdam, quiddam,** *a certain one, a certain thing.*

Adjective: **quīdam, quaedam, quoddam,** *certain.*

Quīdam philosophus hoc dīxit.
A (certain) philosopher said this (i. e., some definite philosopher).

Quaedam scīre dēbēs.
You ought to know certain things.

821 **Note:** Quīdam is often used as an adjective to limit a strong phrase. Translate: *certain, a kind of,* or *as it were.*

Poētae divīnō quōdam spīritū īnflantur.
Poets are inspired by a certain divine breath.
Poets are inspired, as it were, by a divine breath.

ONE . . . OTHER (ANOTHER)

822 **1.** Of more than two:

one . . . another, **alius, a, ud . . . alius, a, ud.**
some . . . others, **aliī, ae, a . . . aliī, ae, a.**

Alius dīvitiās quaerit, alius honōrēs.
One seeks riches, another honors.

Aliī fūgērunt, aliī sē dēdidērunt.
Some fled, others surrendered.

823   2. Of two only:

one . . . *the other*, **alter, altera, alterum** . . . **alter, altera, alterum.**

one (group) . . . *the other (group)*, **alterī, ae, a** . . . **alterī, ae, a.**

> Alter sapientior est, alter fortior.
> *The one is wiser, the other braver.*

> Alterī Caesarī inimīcī sunt, alterī amīcī.
> *The one party is hostile to Caesar, the other party is friendly.*

ONE

824   1. When 'one' refers to one OF TWO, it is generally translated by *alter, altera, alterum.*

> Alter oculus, *one eye*
> (We have only TWO eyes.)

> Alter frāter, *one brother*
> (When there are only TWO brothers.)

825   2. When the English has: "One does one thing, another another," the Latin combines this into one expression, thus:

> *One seeks one thing, another another.*
> Alius aliud quaerit.

> *One praises one person, another another.*
> Alius alium laudat.

> *Some think one thing, others another thing.*
> Aliī alia sentiunt.

826   3. In simple enumerations *alter, altera, alterum* is **used**
for 'the second,' instead of *secundus, a, um.*

Prīma diēs, <u>altera</u> diēs, tertia diēs
The first day, the second day, the third day

OTHER

827   1. 'The other' (of TWO): *alter, altera, alterum.*
'The other group' (of TWO): *alterī, alterae, altera.*

<u>Alter</u> occīsus est.
The other was killed.

<u>Alterī</u> Caesarem adjūvērunt.
The other group helped Caesar.

828   2. 'Others,' in general: *aliī, ae, a.*

Rōmānī <u>aliōs</u> regere scīvērunt.
The Romans knew how to rule others.

829   3. 'The others,' 'the rest,' after a part is removed:
a. cēterī, ae, a, *(all) the rest.*

Hic mīles <u>cēterōs</u> virtūte superat.
This soldier surpasses $\begin{cases} \text{(all) the others} \\ \text{the rest} \end{cases}$ *in courage.*

830   b. reliquī, ae, a, *the others, those remaining.*

Duās legiōnēs in Belgās mīsit, <u>reliquās</u> in hībernās
dēdūxit.
*He sent two legions into Belgium, the <u>others</u> (the
remaining legions) he led into winter quarters.*

EACH

831 1. **Pronoun:** *quisque, quidque,* 'each one,' 'each thing,'
'every one.'

Adjective: *quisque, quaeque, quodque,* 'each,' 'every'
(or *ūnusquisque, ūnaquaeque,* etc.)

832 a. with reflexive pronouns;

Suam quisque patriam dīligit.
Each man ⎫
Every man ⎭ *loves his own country.*

833 b. with ordinal numerals;

Decimum quemque occīdī jussit.
He ordered every tenth man to be killed (lit.: *each
tenth man*).

834 c. with relative and interrogative pronouns and in indirect questions;

Quem quisque dīligit, eum laudat.
Each man praises the one he loves.

Sciō quid quisque dīxerit.
I know what each one said.

835 d. with superlatives **quisque** is nearly ALWAYS in the
singular except when neuter.

Optimus quisque patriam dīligit.
Each best man loves his country.
All the best men love their country.

Optima quaeque quaerimus.
We seek all the best things.

836   2. In other cases *singulī, ae, a* or *ūnusquisque* are generally used for 'each.' Note that *singulī* is always PLURAL.

> Singulī abiērunt.
> Ūnusquisque abiit.
> *Each one went away.*

    3. 'Each,' 'either,' 'both,' when speaking of TWO:

837   a. When the two are spoken of SEPARATELY:

> Pronoun or adjective: **uterque, utraque, utrumque,** *each, either.*

838   b. When the two are spoken of TOGETHER:

> Pronoun or adjective: **ambo, ambae, ambo,** *both.*

> Duo senātōrēs mihi obviam sunt factī; ambōs
> salūtāvī; uterque resalūtāvit.
> *Two senators met me; I greeted them both; each*
> *returned my greeting.*

    4. 'Each other'; 'one another' (reciprocal pronouns):

839   a. alter . . . alter; alius . . . alius;

> Frātrēs alter alterum dīligere dēbent.
> *Brothers ought to love each other.*
> (Lit.: *Brothers ought to love, each the other.*)
> (**Alter** is in apposition, though SINGULAR, with
> the subject; **alterum** is the object of **dīligere**.)

> Gallī alius alium adjuvant.
> *The Gauls help each other.*

840   b. inter sē, inter nōs, inter vōs.

> Obsidēs inter sē dant.
> *They give each other hostages.*
> (Lit.: *They give hostages among themselves.*)

ANYONE; ANY

841 1. **Unemphatic:**

Chiefly after **sī, nisi, num, nē, quō, quantō, quandō, ubi, unde, ut** *(as)*, **cum, alius:**

Pronoun: **quis, quid,** *anyone, anything.*

Adjective: **quī, qua (quae), quod,** *any.*

> Nē quis . . . mīrētur . . .
> *Lest anyone should marvel* . . .

> Sī qua causa est . . .
> *If there is any reason* . . .

2. **Emphatic:**

842 a. In questions expecting a negative answer:

Pronoun: **ecquis, ecquid = num quis.**

Adjective: **ecquis, ecqua, ecquod.**

> Ecquis hoc crēdit?
> *Does anyone believe this?*
> (Answer expected: "No one.")

843 b. In interrogative and negative sentences and **after vix, vērō, quasi, quasi vērō, sine** *(without)*:

Pronoun: **quisquam, quidquam** (or **quicquam**), *anyone, anything.*

Adjective: **ūllus, a, um,** *any.*

> Vōbīs nōn dabō quidquam.
> *I will not give you anything.*

> Sine ūllā spē
> *Without any hope*

844   c. In positive declarative sentences *(anyone at all)*:

     Pronoun: **quīvīs, quaevīs, quidvīs**
                  quīlibet, quaelibet, quidlibet.

     Adjective: **quīvīs, quaevīs, quodvīs**
                  quīlibet, quaelibet, quodlibet.

     <u>Quīvīs</u> hoc facere potest.
     <u>Anyone</u> (at all) can do this.

ADJECTIVES

SPECIAL USES OF ADJECTIVES

Adjectives may be used as nouns. This use is:

1. **Very frequent, especially to designate a general class:**

845   a. in the masculine plural.

> Nostrī fortiter pugnābant.
> *Our men were fighting bravely.*
>
> Fortūna fortēs adjuvat.
> *Fortune helps the brave.*

846   b. in the neuter nominative and accusative plural.

> Vēra dīcit.
> *He speaks the truth* (lit.: *true things*).

2. **Less frequent:**

847   a. in the masculine singular and only to stand for a class.

> Sapiēns omnia sua sēcum portat.
> *The wise man carries all his possessions with him.*

848   b. in the neuter singular, generally of adjectives of the first and second declensions only.

> Vērum dīcit.
> *He speaks the truth.*
>
> Parvō contentus est.
> *He is content with little.*

849   **Latin often uses ADJECTIVES expressing a state of body or soul where the English uses ADVERBS.**

> Mīlitēs in castra tūtī pervēnērunt.
> *The soldiers arrived in the camp safely* (lit.: *safe*).

850   *Ultimus, sōlus, prīmus,* and similar adjectives are often equivalent to a relative clause.

> Prīmus in urbem vēnit.
>
> *He was the first* { *one who came into the city.*
>   { *to come into the city.*
>
> (Lit.: *He came as the first one.*)

851   *Summus,* 'highest'; *medius,* 'middle'; *īmus,* 'lowest'; *infimus,* 'lowest'; *interior,* 'inner'; *intimus,* 'innermost'; *prīmus,* 'first'; *postrēmus,* 'last'; *ultimus,* 'last'; *reliquus,* 'remaining' (generally standing before their noun), often mean PART of the object.

> Mīlitēs in summō colle īnstrūxit.
> *He drew up the soldiers on the top of the hill.*

> Per mediam urbem contendit.
> *He hastened through the middle of the city.*

852   When *multus* is joined to another adjective to modify the same noun *et* is generally used.

> Erant multae et magnae urbēs in Italiā.
> *There were many large cities in Italy.*

COMPARATIVE ADJECTIVES

The Latin comparative may be translated:

853   1. by the English comparative.

> Hoc flūmen lātius est quam Tiberis.
> *This river is wider than the Tiber.*

854   2. by *somewhat* or *too* with the English positive.

> Mōns altior est.
> *The mountain is somewhat high.*

855   **Note:** In expressions like: "He was braver than he was safe," the Latin generally uses the COMPARATIVE in both parts of the comparison.

> Fortior erat quam tūtior.
> *He was braver than he was safe.*

SUPERLATIVE ADJECTIVES

856   **Superlative adjectives are used much more in Latin than in English. They are therefore weaker and may often be translated by 'very' with the English positive or even by the English positive alone.**

> Maximum impetum in eōs fēcērunt.
> *They made a very strong (or strong) attack on them.*

Note:

857   1. To express the ABSOLUTE superlative, the Latin superlative is used with **ūnus, a, um** and **omnium** or simply with **omnium.**

> Hic mōns ūnus omnium altissimus est.
> *This mountain is the (one) highest of all.*

> Hoc flūmen est omnium longissimum.
> *This river is the longest of all.*

858   2. When a superlative modifies the antecedent of a relative it is regularly put into the relative clause.

> Centuriōnem quī fortissimus in castrīs erat mīsit.
> *He sent the bravest centurion who was in the camp.*
> (Not: Centuriōnem fortissimum . . .)

859   3. The adverb **vel,** *very,* is sometimes used to strengthen a superlative.

> Vel maxima virtūs
> *The very greatest courage*

VERBAL NOUNS AND ADJECTIVES

THE SUPINE

1. IN -UM

860   The supine in *-um* may be used to express purpose
after verbs of motion.
It may have a word-object (not a clause-object).
It may be modified by adverbs.

> Lēgātī pācem petītum vēnērunt.
> *Envoys came to seek peace.*

> Eōs ad mē mane salūtātum mīserās.
> *You had sent them to salute me in the morning.*

2. IN -Ū

861   The supine in *-ū* may be used to express RESPECT
after *fās est, nefās est, opus est,* and some adjectives.
It may take only a clause-object (not a word-object).
It may not be modified by an adverb.

> Mīrābile dictū
> *Marvelous to relate*

> Nefās est dictū miseram esse tālem senectūtem.
> *It is criminal to call such an old age miserable.*

Note:

862   1. The only supines in **-ū** in common use are: **dictū,** *to say;*
factū, *to do;* **audītū,** *to hear;* **cognitū,** *to learn;* **vīsū,**
to see; **intellēctū,** *to understand.*

863   2. The adjectives which take a supine in **-ū** are especially:
**facilis (difficilis), pulcher, crēdibilis (incrēdibilis),
bonus (malus).**

THE GERUND

864   The gerund is a verbal noun. It has all the cases except the nominative.

As a VERB: 1. It is modified by adverbs and takes objects.

                2. It is always active in meaning.

As a NOUN it is used in all the case usages of nouns, *but:*

1. The accusative of the gerund is used chiefly after **ad** or **in**; not as the object of a transitive verb.

2. The ablative is never used with **sine**, *without,* or **cum**, *with.*

Genitive: Pugnandī cupidī sunt.
                They are eager for fighting.
                They are eager to fight.

                Pugnandī causā vēnērunt.
                They came for the sake of fighting.

Dative: Scrībendō sē dedit.
                He devoted himself to writing.

Accusative: Ad explōrandum missus est.
                He was sent for reconnoitering.
                He was sent to reconnoiter.

Ablative: Dē bene scrībendō locūtus est.
                He spoke about writing well.

                Mēns cōgitandō excolitur.
                The mind is developed by thinking.

THE GERUNDIVE

THE GERUNDIVE CONSTRUCTION

865   The gerundive is a PASSIVE VERBAL ADJECTIVE. As a VERB it expresses action and may be modified by adverbs and adverbial phrases.

As an ADJECTIVE it agrees with a noun or noun-equivalent.

The gerundive has two general uses:

1. As an attributive adjective in the oblique cases. In this use it directly modifies a noun and has the meaning of:

866   a. a present passive participle.

> ponte faciendō
> *by building a bridge*
> (Lit.: *by a bridge being built*)

867   b. a future passive participle.

> dē ponte faciendō
> *about building a bridge*
> (Lit.: *about a bridge to be built*)

2. To express obligation or necessity:

868   a. as a predicate adjective with **sum**. (See Nos. 878-884.)

869   b. as an attributive adjective.

> Hostis nōn metuendus
> *An enemy not to be feared*

THE ATTRIBUTIVE GERUNDIVE AS A
SUBSTITUTE FOR THE GERUND

870   When the gerund would have an ACCUSATIVE OB-
JECT the gerundive construction is generally used instead of the gerund.

EXAMPLE: They are desirous of seeing the city.

The gerund construction would be: Urbem videndī cupidī
sunt. Since the **urbem** would be an accusative object the
construction is changed to the gerundive as follows:

1. The accusative object is put in the case of the gerund.

Urbis (The gerund **videndī** is genitive.)

2. The gerundive is made to agree with it.

Urbis videndae

The complete sentence now is:

Urbis videndae cupidī sunt.
(Lit.: *They are eager for the city to-be-seen.*)
They are desirous of seeing the city.
They are eager to see the city.

EXAMPLE: They were sent to capture the town.

The gerund construction would be:

Ad capiendum urbem missī sunt.
They were sent for capturing the city.

The gerundive construction:

Ad urbem capiendam missī sunt.
They were sent for the city to-be-captured.

Note:

871   1. The gerundive construction should always be used when the gerund with an object would be in the dative or would follow a preposition.

> Ad urbem videndam vēnit.
> *He came to see the city.*
> (The gerund would be: ad urbem <u>videndum</u>, which should never be used.)

872   2. The gerundive construction after **ad** or **causā** *(w. gen.)* is a common way of expressing purpose.

> *They came to see the leader.*
> Ad ducem videndum vēnērunt.
> *They came to seize the bridge.*
> Pontis capiendī causā vēnērunt.

    3. The gerundive construction is NOT used:

873   a. when the object of the gerund is a neuter pronoun or adjective.

> Vērum investīgandī causā
> *For the sake of discovering the truth*

874   b. when a series of **-ōrums** or **-ārums** would result.

> *For the sake of taking up these arms*
> (Gerundive would be: <u>Hōrum armōrum capiendōrum</u> causā.)
> Haec arma capiendī causā

875   4. As a rule only transitive verbs can be used in the gerundive. **Ūtor, fruor, fungor, potior,** however, which were transitive in old Latin, are regularly used in this gerundive construction.

> In fungendō mūnere
> *In performing the duty*
> (Lit.: *In the duty-being-performed*)

876   5. DEPONENT verbs are used in this gerundive construction.

> In eīs sequendīs multās hōrās cōnsūmpsērunt.
>
> *They consumed many hours* $\begin{cases} \textit{in pursuing them.} \\ \textit{in them-being-pursued.} \end{cases}$

877   6. The forms meī, tuī, suī, nostrī, vestrī are always used with the gerundive in the singular agreeing with them, irrespective of gender or number.

> Nostrī servandī causā in castra fūgimus.
> *We fled into the camp to save ourselves.*
> (Nostrī refers to *we* in the verb fūgimus but the gerundive is servandī not servandōrum.)
>
> Mulierēs suī cōnservandī causā fūgērunt.
> *The women fled to save themselves.*
> (Cōnservandī not cōnservandārum is used, although suī refers to the FEMININE PLURAL mulierēs.)

THE GERUNDIVE AS A PREDICATE ADJECTIVE WITH *SUM*

878   To express OBLIGATION or NECESSITY
the gerundive may be used as a predicate adjective
with the proper form of the verb *sum*.

> Deus laudandus est.
> *God is to-be-praised.*
> *God should be praised.*
> *God ought to be praised.*
> *God must be praised.*
> *God has to be praised.*
> *It is necessary to praise God.*

Vōs laudandī nōn estis.
You should not be praised.

Hoc faciendum nōn fuit.
This was not to-be-done.
This should not have been done.

879   **Note:** As a predicate adjective **laudandus, a, um** follows
the usual rule of agreement for predicate adjectives,
Nos. 474-476.

880   **With transitive verbs use the gerundive personally.**

Deus laudandus est.
God is to be praised.

Dīxī Deum laudandum esse.
I said God should be praised.

Rogāvit num Deus laudandus esset.
He asked whether God should be praised.

881   **With intransitive verbs**
or with transitive verbs without a subject
use the gerundive impersonally.

(If an intransitive verb has a subject in English, put the
subject in the case governed by the verb.)

Transitive verb without a subject:

Vincendum est.
(It must be conquered.)
It is necessary to conquer.

Genitive verb:

Meī oblīvīscendum nōn est.
I should not be forgotten.

Dative verb:

> Deō serviendum est.
> *God should be served.*

Ablative verb:

> Dīligentiā ūtendum est.
> *Care should be used.*

Intransitive verb in the accusative with the infinitive:

> Dīxī Deō serviendum esse.
> *I said that God should be served.*

Intransitive verb in a subordinate clause:

> Rogāvit num Deō serviendum esset.
> *He asked whether God should be served.*

882   **To express the AGENT with the gerundive use the DATIVE;**
but *ab (ā)* and the ablative when there is another dative in the same clause.

> Deus nōbīs laudandus est.
> *We should praise God.*
> *We ought to praise God.*
> *We are to praise God.*
> *We must praise God.*
> *It is necessary that we praise God.*
> *It is necessary for us to praise God.*
> *God should be praised by us.*
> *God ought to be praised by us.*

> Dīligentiā nōbīs ūtendum est.
> *We should use care.*

Deō ā <u>nōbīs</u> serviendum est.
We should serve God.
(**Ā nōbīs** is used because of the dative **Deō.**)

Dīxī Deō ā <u>nōbīs</u> serviendum esse.
I said we should serve God.

Dīxī Deum <u>nōbīs</u> laudandum esse.
I said we should praise God.

Rogāvit num Deus <u>nōbīs</u> laudandus esset.
He asked whether we should praise God.

Rogāvit num Deō ā <u>nōbīs</u> serviendum esset.
He asked whether we should serve God.

THE GERUNDIVE AS A PREDICATE ADJECTIVE WITH OTHER VERBS

883 *Dō*, 'I give'; *trādō*, 'I hand over'; *cūrō*, 'I take care of';
suscipiō, 'I undertake'; and the like
may take an accusative object
and a gerundive in agreement.

Urbem mīlitibus dīripiendam trādidit.
He handed over the city to the soldiers to plunder.
(Lit.: *the city to-be-plundered.*)

Classem aedificandam suscēpī.
I undertook the building of a fleet.
(Lit.: *I undertook a fleet to-be-built.*)

884 **Note:** In the passive, the object will become the subject
nominative and the gerundive will agree with it.

<u>Urbs</u> mīlitibus <u>dīripienda</u> trādita est.
The <u>city</u> was handed over to the soldiers <u>to be plundered.</u>

TENSES OF THE INFINITIVE AND THE PARTICIPLE

TENSE BY RELATION

885   1. The PRESENT infinitive and the PRESENT participle express action as GOING ON AT THE TIME of the action of the finite verb in their clause.

Infinitive: Sciō tē pugnāre.
I know that you are fighting.
(You are now fighting and I now know it.)

Scīvī tē pugnāre.
I knew that you were fighting.
(You were then fighting and I then knew it.)

Participle: Ōrāns Deum laudō.
Praying I praise God.
(I praise God while praying.)

Eōs pugnantēs hortātus est.
He encouraged them fighting (as they fought).
(He encouraged them at the time when they were fighting.)

Pugnāns vulnerātus est.
He was wounded (while) fighting.
(He was wounded at the time when he was fighting.)

Servīs clāmantibus, dominus occīsus est.
The master was killed while the slaves shouted.
(The slaves were shouting at the same time that the master was killed.)

886   2. The PERFECT infinitive and the PERFECT participle express action as COMPLETED BEFORE the action of the verb in their clause.

Infinitive: Sciō tē hoc fēcisse.
I know that you did this.
(i. e., *You did it before and I now know it.*)

Scīvī tē hoc fēcisse.
I knew that you had done this.
(i. e., *You did it before I knew it.*)

Participle: Mīlitēs īnstrūctī impetum sustinent.
The soldiers, having been drawn up, are withstanding the attack.
(i. e., *They have been drawn up and are NOW withstanding the attack.*)

Mīlitēs īnstrūctī impetum sustinuērunt.
The soldiers, having been drawn up, withstood the attack.
(i. e., *They were drawn up and then withstood the attack.*)

Urbe captā, cōpiam frūmentī habēmus.
The city having been captured, we have a supply of grain.
(i. e., *After the capture of the city we now have a supply of grain.*)

Urbe captā, hostēs sē dēdidērunt.
The city having been captured, the enemy surrendered.
(i. e., *The city was captured and then they surrendered.*)

887 3. The FUTURE infinitive and the FUTURE participle express action which WILL TAKE PLACE AFTER the action of the verb in their clause.

Infinitive: Sciō tē Gallōs victūrum esse.
I know that you will conquer the Gauls.

Scīvī tē Gallōs victūrum esse.
I knew that you would conquer the Gauls.

Participle: Itūrus haec dīcit.
Being about to go, he says these things.

Itūrus haec dīxit.
Being about to go, he said these things.

THE INFINITIVE

888　　The infinitive is a **VERBAL NOUN**.

As a **VERB** it has **TENSE** and **VOICE**, may take **OBJECTS**, both direct and indirect, and may be modified by adverbs or adverbial expressions.

As a **NOUN** it may be used as a **NEUTER** noun in noun constructions but only in the nominative and accusative cases. An adjective or pronoun may agree with the infinitive in the neuter singular. (See first example under No. 889.)

THE INFINITIVE IN NOUN CONSTRUCTIONS

889　　1. The infinitive may be used as **SUBJECT, OBJECT, PREDICATE NOUN**, and (rarely) appositive.

As subject :　Ōrāre est bonum.
To pray ⎫
Praying ⎭ *is good.*

As predicate noun :　Laudāre Deum est ōrāre.
To praise God is to pray.

As object :　Pugnāre timent
They fear to fight.

2. This use of the infinitive is very common:

890　　　　a. with nouns and neuter adjectives with **est, erat,** etc.

Mōs fuit fortēs laudāre.
It was the custom to praise the brave.

Nōn est malum sē dēfendere.
It is not bad to defend oneself.[1]

---

[1]*Oneself*, the object of the infinitive, is an indefinite reflexive (No. 801).

891   b. after such impersonal verbs as **piget,** *it annoys;*
              pudet, *it shames;* **oportet,**[1] *it behooves;* **licet,**[1] *it is
              allowed;* **necesse est,**[1] *it is necessary;* **praestat,** *it is
              better;* **placet,** *it pleases;* **convenit,** *it is becoming.*

              Īre necesse est.
              It is necessary to go.

              Quis tē dēfendere audet?
              Who dares to defend you?

892   c. after verbs which require further action by the same
              subject to complete their meaning, such as **possum,**
              am able; **dēbeō,** *ought;* **volō,** *wish;* **nōlō,** *am un-
              willing;* **mālō,** *prefer;* **cupiō,** *desire;* **studeō,** *am
              eager;* **contendō,** *strive;* **soleō,** *am accustomed;* **in-
              cipiō,** *begin;* **cōnor,** *try;* **audeō,** *dare;* **doceō,** *teach;*
              discō, *learn;* **dubitō,** *hesitate;* **oblīvīscor,** *forget;*
              timeō, *fear;* **dēcernō,** *determine;* etc.

              Mīlitēs Rōmānī fortiter pugnāre solēbant.
              Roman soldiers were accustomed to fight bravely.

              Exercitus superārī nōn potuit.
              The army could not be conquered.

---

[1]These verbs may also take the subjunctive without *ut* (No. 641).

893 **3. When the SENSE requires it, the infinitive may have a SUBJECT IN THE ACCUSATIVE CASE.**[1]

As subject: Populōs inter sē pugnāre malum est.
That nations fight among themselves is bad.

As object: Caesar eōs in castrīs manēre jussit.
Caesar ordered them to remain in the camp.

Note:

894 **1.** A predicate adjective or predicate noun after the infinitive agrees with the word, expressed or understood, to which it refers.

Oportet mīlitēs esse parātōs.
It behooves soldiers to be prepared.

Semper esse parātum bonum est (**hominem** understood).
It is good to be always ready.
(It is good that a man be always ready.)

Puerī bonī esse possunt.
Boys can be good.
(**Bonī** here REFERS to **puerī** and hence must agree with it.)

895 **2. Jubeō**, *order*, **vetō**, *forbid*, **sinō**, *allow,* are used personally in the passive.

Active: Eōs pugnāre jussit.
He ordered them to fight.

Passive: Eī pugnāre jussī sunt.
They were ordered to fight.

896 **3.** Note that the infinitive in these constructions (Nos. 889-895) is regularly in the PRESENT tense unless (rarely) the SENSE demands a different tense.

Prō patriā pugnāvisse pulchrum est.
It is glorious to have fought for one's fatherland.

---

[1]This is common especially with *volō*, 'wish,' *nōlō*, 'am unwilling,' *mālō*, 'prefer,' *cupiō*, 'desire,' *patior*, 'allow'; with the active voice of *jubeō*, 'order,' *vetō*, 'forbid,' *sinō*, 'permit'; and with verbs of emotion (No. 715).

THE ACCUSATIVE WITH THE INFINITIVE AFTER VERBS OF SAYING, THINKING, AND THE LIKE

897   Verbs of 'saying,' 'thinking,' 'perceiving,' and the like take the ACCUSATIVE WITH THE INFINITIVE. The subject of the infinitive is in the ACCUSATIVE; the verb is in the infinitive; the tense of the infinitive is determined strictly by the rule: Tense by Relation (Nos. 885-887).

Sciō tē <u>pugnāre.</u>
I know that you are fighting.

898   In this use the accusative with the infinitive is equivalently a NOUN CLAUSE.

Audīvī tē pugnāre.
I heard that you were fighting.

Putō tē pugnātūrum esse.
I think that you will fight.

Sciō tē pugnāvisse.
I know that you $\begin{cases} \textit{fought.} \\ \textit{were fighting.} \end{cases}$

Scīvī tē pugnāvisse.
I knew that you had fought.

Putāvī tē pugnātūrum esse.
I thought that you would fight.

Sciō eōs vincī.
I know that they are being conquered.

Sciō Gallōs ā Rōmānīs victōs esse.
I know that Gauls were conquered by the Romans.

Note:

899   1. The future infinitive active is formed with the future participle active and the present infinitive of **sum, esse.** The perfect infinitive passive is formed with the perfect participle passive and the present infinitive of **sum, esse.** In both cases the participle is used in a compound tense like a predicate adjective and must therefore agree with the subject accusative.

> Dīcō mīlitēs nostrōs victūrōs esse.
> *I say that our men will conquer.*

> Dīcō hanc gentem pugnātūram esse.
> *I say that this nation will fight.*

> Audīvī Rōmam oppugnātam esse.
> *I heard that Rome had been attacked.*

> Sciō Rōmānōs victōs nōn esse.
> *I know that the Romans were not conquered.*

900   2. A predicate adjective in the accusative with the infinitive will of course agree with the subject accusative.

> Dīcō hanc cīvitātem līberam semper futūram esse.
> *I say that this state will always be free.*

> Sciō Deum esse bonum.
> *I know that God is good.*

   3. When the verb of *saying, thinking, perceiving, etc.,* is in the PASSIVE:

901   a. If it is a COMPOUND tense, it is generally used impersonally and takes the accusative with the infinitive.

> Trāditum est prīmōs rēgēs bonōs fuisse.
> *It has been handed down that the first kings were good.*

902　　**b.** If it is an UNCOMPOUNDED tense, it is generally used personally and takes the infinitive, tense by relation.

> Rēx dīcitur fūgisse.
> *The king is said to have fled.*
> *It is said that the king has fled.*
>
> Ille vir dīcitur esse rēx.
> *That man is said to be the king.*
> *It is said that that man is the king.*
>
> Dīcitur occīsus esse.
> *He is said to have been killed.*
> *It is said that he has been killed.*
>
> Putātur rēx futūrus esse.
> *It is thought that he will be king.*
> (Lit.: *He is thought to be about to be king.*)

903　　**Note:** **Videor,** *seem,* always follows No. 902, but **vidētur mihi,** etc., *it seems well to me,* etc. *(I decide)* is always used impersonally and takes the (accusative with) the infinitive. **Crēditur,** *it is believed,* regularly takes the accusative with the infinitive.

> Eum audīre vīsus sum.
> *I seemed to hear him.*
>
> Nōbīs vīsum est $\begin{cases} \text{lēgātōs mittere.} \\ \text{lēgātōs mittī.} \end{cases}$
> *We decided to send envoys.*
>
> Crēditur eum esse rēgem.
> *It is believed that he is a king.*

THE INFINITIVE IN EXCLAMATIONS

904 The accusative with the infinitive is sometimes used in exclamations and exclamatory questions.

Tē hoc nōn vidēre!
(The idea) that you did not see this!

Mātrem mortuam esse?
Mother dead?

HISTORICAL INFINITIVE

905 The present infinitive is sometimes used for vividness in narration instead of the imperfect indicative. The subject is in the nominative. This infinitive regularly occurs in a series of two or more verbs; rarely in one single verb.

Hostēs ex omnibus partibus impetum facere; tēla conjicere.
The enemy were attacking from all sides; they were hurling darts.

THE INFINITIVE AFTER ADJECTIVES

906 The infinitive is used in poetry to complete the meaning of many adjectives WHICH DO NOT TAKE THE INFINITIVE IN PROSE. (Parātus, a, um, *ready,* and assuētus, a, um, *accustomed,* are used with the infinitive in good prose.)

Audāx omnia perpetī
Bold to endure everything

THE PARTICIPLE

907 1. The participle is a verbal adjective.

As a VERB it has VOICE AND TENSE, takes OBJECTS, both direct and indirect, and is MODIFIED by adverbs and adverbial phrases.

As an ADJECTIVE it modifies nouns or noun-equivalents and follows the regular rule for agreement of adjectives, Nos. 474-478.

908 2. The TENSE of participles is always according to the rule: TENSE BY RELATION.

909 3. There are only three participles in Latin:

Present participle active: **laudāns,** *praising*

Future participle active: **laudātūrus, a, um,** *(being) about to praise*

Perfect participle passive: **laudātus, a, um,** *praised, having been praised*

910 Note: DEPONENT verbs alone have a perfect participle ACTIVE; **locūtus, a, um,** *having spoken* (NOT *having been spoken*).

911 4. A participle may be used to modify any noun or pronoun in any construction.

Gallōs captōs interfēcit.
He killed the captured Gauls.

Hāc rē commōtus, fūgit.
Alarmed by this affair, he fled.

Frūmentum Gallīs captīs dedit.
He gave grain to the captured Gauls.

Caesar propter lēgātōs occīsōs bellum gessit.
Caesar because of the murdered envoys waged war.

Mīlitum occīsōrum virtūtem laudāvit.
He praised the courage of the slaughtered soldiers.

Magna frūmentī cōpia in urbe captā erat.
There was a great supply of grain in the captured city.

Haec pollicitus abiit.
Having promised these things, he went away.

Rēgem profectum interfēcērunt.
They killed the king after he had set out (lit.: *the king having set out*).

Pugnāns occīsus est.
He was killed (while) fighting.

Rēgem proficīscentem interfēcērunt.
They killed the king as he was setting out (lit.: *the king setting out*).

Moritūrus haec dīxit.
He said these things as he was about to die (lit.: *being about to die*).

Rēgem profectūrum interfēcērunt.
They killed the king as he was about to set out (lit.: *the king being about to set out*).

THE ABLATIVE ABSOLUTE

912 The ablative absolute consists of:

a noun
or
pronoun
} in the ablative and a {
participle,
adjective,
or noun
} in agreement.

The noun or pronoun in the **ABLATIVE ABSOLUTE**
may not express the same person or thing
as another noun or pronoun in the same clause;
tense of the participle by relation (Nos. 885-887).

Urbe captā, Caesar pācem fēcit.
The city having been captured, Caesar made peace.

Caesare duce, Rōmānī hostēs vīcērunt.
Caesar (being) leader, the Romans conquered the enemy.

Mē invītō, hoc fēcit.
I being unwilling, he did this.

Duce moritūrō, mīlitēs fūgērunt.
The leader being about to die, the soldiers fled.

913 In the examples given above the ablative absolute is translated by the English nominative absolute. As this construction is generally avoided in English, the ablative absolute
should generally be translated by other clauses and phrases.
The ablative absolute is a general adverbial construction
and may take the place of many different kinds of clauses
and phrases. Study these examples:

Hīs dictīs, abiit.
Lit.: *These things having been said, he went away.*
Having said these things, he went away (ACTIVE Eng-
lish participle).
When (after) these things had been said, he went away.

Caesare absente, hostēs ad castra advēnērunt.
Lit.: *Caesar being absent, the enemy arrived at the camp.*
While Caesar was away, the enemy arrived at the camp.
In Caesar's absence, the enemy arrived at the camp.

Caesare absente, tamen Rōmānī nōn fūgērunt.
Lit.: *Caesar being absent, the Romans nevertheless did not flee.*
Although Caesar was absent, the Romans did not flee.

Eō interfectō, mīlitēs fugient.
Lit.: *He having been killed, the soldiers will flee.*
If he is killed, the soldiers will flee.

Tē duce, hostēs vincēmus.
Lit.: *You being leader, we shall conquer the enemy.*
With you as leader, we shall conquer the enemy.
Under your leadership, we shall conquer the enemy.
Led by you, we shall conquer the enemy.

914 **To translate a perfect participle active into Latin; either a deponent verb must be used or the sentence must be changed so that the participle is passive. (Do not change the sense!)**

Having said this, Caesar went away.
(*Having said this* is a perfect participle ACTIVE.)

1. Using a deponent:
   Caesar, haec locūtus, abiit.

2. Changing into the PASSIVE:

   This having been said, Caesar went away.
   Hīs dictīs, Caesar abiit.

RULES FOR PLACE

WHERE?

915   To express place *WHERE*
use *in* and the ablative;
but locative[1] of names of towns and small islands
and *domī, rūrī, humī.*

     Nōn Rōmae sed in Galliā
     Not at Rome but in Gaul

WHENCE?

916   To express place *FROM WHICH*
use *ex, dē, ab* and the ablative;
but ablative alone of names of towns and small islands
and *domō, rūre, humō.*

     Nōn solum Rōmā sed ex Italiā
     Not only from Rome, but out of Italy

WHITHER?

917   To express place *TO WHICH*
use *ad* or *in* and the accusative;
but accusative alone of names of towns and small islands
and *domum, rūs.*

     Rōmam in Italiam
     Into Italy to Rome

---

[1]See No. 30.

918

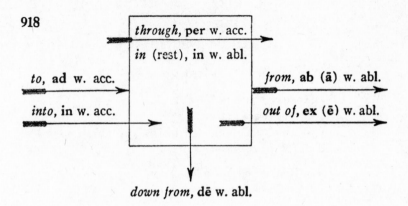

down from, **dē** w. abl.

RULES FOR TIME

HOW LONG?

919　To express time *HOW LONG* use the accusative.

Duās hōrās pugnāvērunt.

They fought $\begin{cases} \text{for two hours.} \\ \text{during two hours.} \\ \text{two hours.} \end{cases}$

WHEN?

920　To express time *WHEN* use the ablative.

Quartō diē advēnērunt.

$\left.\begin{array}{l} \textit{The fourth day} \\ \textit{On the fourth day} \end{array}\right\}$ *they arrived.*

921　**Note:** With words not expressing time of themselves **in is** generally used.

> *In war*
> In bellō (But: Bellō Pūnicō secundō)

WITHIN?

922　To express time *WITHIN WHICH* use the ablative.

Quīnque diēbus veniet.

He will come $\left\{\begin{array}{l} \textit{in} \\ \textit{within} \end{array}\right\}$ *five days.*

HOW LONG AGO?

923   To express time *HOW LONG AGO* use *abhinc* with
the accusative.

Abhinc annōs decem
Ten years ago

HOW LONG BEFORE OR AFTER?

924   To express time *HOW LONG BEFORE OR AFTER:*

1. Use ablative with *ante* or *post* as adverbs.

Multīs post annīs (**post** = adverb)
Many years afterwards

2. Use ablative together with *ante* or *post* as prepositions with accusative.

Paulō ante proelium (**ante** = preposition)
Shortly before the battle

Multīs annīs post mortem ējus (**post** = preposition)
Many years after his death

3. Use *ante* or *post* as prepositions with accusative.

Post multōs annōs (**post** = preposition)

PREPOSITIONS

925 Prepositional phrases are regularly used in Latin as ADVERBIAL phrases ONLY. In English prepositional phrases are frequently used as adjectival phrases. When translating an adjectival prepositional phrase into Latin, a verb must usually be added.

> *The war with the Gauls was difficult.*

> *With the Gauls* is an adjectival prepositional phrase because it modifies the NOUN *war*. Hence, a verb must be added in Latin.

> Bellum cum Gallīs <u>gestum</u> erat difficile.
> *The war <u>waged</u> with the Gauls was difficult.*
> *(With the Gauls* is now an adverbial phrase because it modifies the VERB *waged.)*

926 Note: Prepositional phrases, however, are frequently used as adjectives in Latin:

927   1. with nouns expressing an ACTION or an EMOTION.

> Meam in tē voluntātem cognōvistī.
> *You know my good will towards you.*
> Fuga <u>ab urbe</u> subitō fit.
> *The flight from the city happens suddenly.*

928   2. in expressions of time and place.

> Post proelium <u>in prōvinciā</u> Caesar in Italiam contendit.
> *After the battle <u>in the province</u> Caesar hastened into Italy.*

929   **3.** with the phrases introduced by **sine** or **cum**.

Homō sine amīcīs beātus esse nōn potest.

A man without friends cannot be happy.

930   **4.** when the prepositional phrase expresses the whole (No. 692), the material, or the source [**dē, ex (ē), ab (ā)**].

Ūnus ē mīlitibus haec dīxit.

One of (from) the soldiers said this.

931   **5.** when the prepositional phrase can be enclosed between the noun and its modifier.

Cicerōnis dē amīcitiā liber

Cicero's book about friendship

(Cicero's essay on friendship)

ab,[1] **ā and the ablative:**

932   **1.** *from* (of place or time).

ab urbe, *from the city*

ā pueritiā, *from boyhood*

933   **2.** *by* (agent).

ā Caesare laudātus, *praised by Caesar*

ad and the accusative:

934   **1.** *to, towards.*

ad urbem, *to the city*

935   **2.** *near, at.*

ad Rōmam, *near Rome*

ad flūmen, *at the river*

936   **3.** *till, toward* (of time).

ad vesperum, *till evening*

---

[1] *Ā* only before consonants; *ab* before any letter, but rarely before *b, p, f, v, m.*

937 **4.** *for* (purpose).

   ventus ad nāvigandum idōneus, *a good breeze for sailing*

938 **5.** *about* (with numbers).

   ad ducentōs, *about 200*

adversus and the accusative:

939 **1.** *opposite, towards.*

   adversus montem īre, *to go towards the mountain*

940 **2.** *against.*

   adversus hostem, *against the enemy*

941 **3.** *towards* (of feelings, *etc.*).

   Jūstitia etiam adversus īnfimōs servanda est.
   Justice must be observed even towards the most lowly.

942 **ante** and the accusative: *before* (of place or time).

   ante castra, *before (facing) the camp*
   ante lūcem, *before dawn*

apud and the accusative:

943 **1.** *among, in the presence of.*

   Apud senātum verba fēcit.
   He spoke in the presence of (before) the senate.

944 **2.** *in the works of.*

   apud Cicerōnem, *in (the writings of) Cicero*

945 **3.** *at the house of.*

   apud tē, *at your house*

946 *circā* and the accusative: *around, about* (of place or time).

circā flūmina, *around rivers*
circā eandem hōram, *about the same hour*

947 *circiter* and the accusative: *about.*

circiter merīdiem, *about noon*

948 *circum* and the accusative: *around* (of place).

circum forum, *around the forum*
circum eum, *around him*

949 *citrā* and the accusative; *cis* and the accusative: *(on) this side of.*

citrā Rhēnum, *this side of the Rhine*
cis Alpēs, *this side of the Alps*

950 *cōram* and the ablative: *in the presence of, before.*

cōram rēge, *in the presence of the king*

cum and the ablative:

951 1. *with* (accompaniment, union).

tēcum, *with you*

952 2. *with* (manner).

cum celeritāte, *with speed*

dē and the ablative:

953 1. *about, concerning, of* (subject matter).

Dē hāc rē locūtus sum. *I spoke of this.*

954   2. *down from, from.*
      dē mūrō, *down from the wall*

955   3. *of, from* (partitive).
      paucī dē nostrīs, *a few of our men*

956   4. *for, owing to, according to.*
      quā dē causā, *and for this reason*
      dē mōre, *according to custom*

957   **ergā** and the accusative: *towards, for* (generally of friendly feelings).

      summa ergā nōs benevolentia, *great kindness towards us*

ex,[1] **ē and the ablative:**

958   1. *out of, from* (of place, material, or time).
      ex urbe, *out of the city*
      ex argīllā factum, *made of clay*
      ex illō diē, *from that day*

959   2. *of* (partitive).
      ūnus ex captīvīs, *one of the captives*

960   **extrā** and the accusative: *outside (of).*
      extrā fīnēs, *outside the border*

in:

961   1. **with the ablative:** *in, on* (rest).
      in castrīs, *in the camp*
      in ponte, *on the bridge*

---

[1] *Ē* only before consonants; *ex* before any letter, but rarely before *b, p, f, v, m.*

2. **with the accusative:**

962   a. *into, onto* (motion).

in Galliam, *into Gaul*
in nāvēs, *onto the ships*

963   b. *for, till* (of time).

Concilium in posterum diem distulit. *He put off the council till the next day.*
in futūrum, *for the future*

964   c. *for, against.*

amor in patriam, *patriotism*
ōrātiō in Catilīnam habita, *the speech against Catiline*

965   **īnfrā and the accusative:** *below, beneath.*

īnfrā sīdera, *beneath the stars*

inter and the accusative:

966   1. *between* (of place).

inter castra et flūmen, *between the camp and the river*

967   2. *among.*

Inter omnēs cōnstat. *It is agreed on among all.*

968   3. *during* (time).

inter bellum, *during the war*

969   **intrā and the accusative:** *within* (motion, rest, time).

intrā fīnēs esse, *to be within the borders*
tēla intrā mūnītiōnēs conjicere, *to hurl darts within the defense works*
intrā decem diēs, *within ten days*

970   *jūxtā* and the accusative: *near*.

jūxtā arborem, *near a tree*

ob and the accusative:

971   1. *before* (of place).

ob oculōs versārī, *to keep (be) before one's eyes*

972   2. *for, on account of*.

ob hanc causam, *for (on account of) this reason*

973   *penes* and the accusative: *in the power of, under the control of*.

penes tē, *in your power*

per and the accusative:

974   1. *through, throughout* (of place or time).

per prōvinciam, *through the province*
per orbem terrārum, *throughout the world*
per hiemem, *throughout (during) the winter*

975   2. *through, by* (intermediate agent).

per explōrātōrēs, *through scouts*
per nuntium, *by a messenger*

976   3. *through* (means).

per litterās cognōscere, *to learn by means of a letter*

977   4. *owing to* (cause).

Per annī tempus iter facere nōn possum. *Owing to the season I cannot travel.*

978   5. *by* (in oaths).

Per deōs jūrō. *I swear by the gods.*

post and the accusative:

979   1. *behind* (of place).

post castra, *behind the camp*

980   2. *after* (of time).

post proelium, *after the battle*

prae and the ablative:

981   1. *before (in preference to).*

prae omnibus, *before all*

982   2. *for* (preventing cause).

Prae timōre loquī nōn potuit. *He could not speak for fear.*

983   3. *in comparison with.*

Gallīs prae magnitūdine corporum suōrum brevitās nostra contemptuī est. *Our small stature is contemptible to the Gauls in comparison with their own size.*

praeter and the accusative:

984   1. *past, by, beyond* (of place).

praeter castra īre, *to go by the camp*

985   2. *contrary to, beyond, except.*

praeter cōnsuētūdinem, *contrary to custom*
praeter modum, *beyond measure*
praeter tē nēmō, *no one except you*

prō and the ablative:

986   1. *before, in front of (with back towards).*

prō castrīs collocātus, *stationed before the camp*

987   2. *on behalf of.*

prō patriā morī. *to die for one's country*

988   3. *instead of, in place of.*

    prō parente, *instead of a father*

989   4. *in return for.*

    prō beneficiīs, *in return for favors*

990   5. *in accordance with, in proportion to, in view of.*

    prō tuā benevolentiā, *in accordance with your kindness*

991   ***prope*** and the accusative: *near (to).*

    prope mūrum, *near the wall*

992   ***propter*** and the accusative: *on account of, because of.*

    propter timōrem, *because of fear*

    secundum and the accusative:

993   1. *along.*

    secundum flūmen, *along the river*

994   2. *after (following).*

    secundum proelium, *after the battle*

995   3. *according to.*

    secundum reī nātūram, *according to the nature of the thing*

996   ***sine*** and the ablative: *without.*

    sine veste, *without a garment*
    sine spē, *without hope*

sub:

1. **with the ablative:**

997   a. *under* (place where, rest).

> sub monte cōnsīdere, *to encamp at the foot of the mountain*
> sub arbore, *under a tree*

998   b. *towards* (of time).

> sub vespere, *towards evening*

2. **with the accusative:**

999   a. *under* (motion).

> sub jugum mittere, *to send under the yoke*
> sub montem succēdere, *to come to the foot of the mountain*

1000   b. *at* (time).

> sub noctem, *at (just before) nightfall*

1001 **super and the accusative:** *above* (motion, rest).

> super rūpem stāre, *to stand above the cliff*
> super terram volāre, *to fly above the earth*

1002 **suprā and the accusative:** *above, beyond.*

> suprā sīdera, *above the stars*

1003 **tenus (post-positive) and the ablative:** *as far as.*

> flūmine tenus, *as far as the river*

1004   *trāns* and the accusative: *across* (motion, rest).

Caesar exercitum trāns Rhēnum dūxit. *Caesar led his army across the Rhine.*

Germānī trāns Rhēnum incolunt. *The Germans dwell across the Rhine.*

METHOD OF DIAGRAMMING

1005   1. **Simple sentence:** Mīles optimus fortiter pugnat.

```
mīles   |   pugnat
____|_____
   | optimus | fortiter
   |_____|_____
```

1006   2. **Predicate noun or adjective:** Caesar est imperātor.

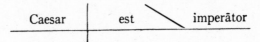

1007   3. **Direct object:** Brūtus Caesarem interfēcit.

```
Brūtus | interfēcit | Caesarem
```

1008   4. **Two accusative objects:** Tē linguam Latīnam doceō.

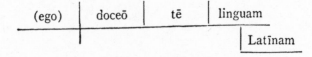

1009   5. **Accusative object and predicate accusative:**

Tē imperātōrem appellō.

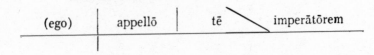

1010   6. **Dative (genitive, ablative) object:** <u>Deō</u> servīmus.

(nōs)	servīmus	Deō

1011   7. **Indirect object:** Caesar arma <u>mīlitibus</u> dedit.

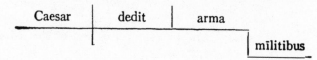

1012   8. **Compound sentence:** Caesar vīvit et nōs vīvimus.

Caesar	vīvit		et	nōs	vīvimus

9. **Complex sentences:**

   a. **Noun clauses**

1013   1. *As subject :* Accidit ut lūna esset plēna.

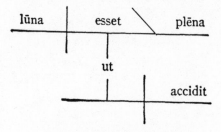

1014   2. *As object:* Dīxit sē ventūrum esse.

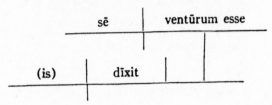

1015   3. *As predicate noun:* Mōs est ut nōs eō **conve-**
niāmus.

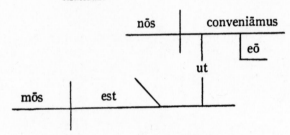

1016   b. **Adverb clauses:** Edō ut vīvam.

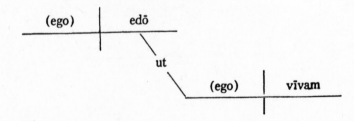

1017 c. **Adjective clauses:** Mīlitēs quī nūper cōnscrīptī erant vēnērunt.

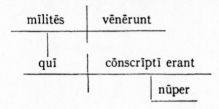

APPENDIX

PRONUNCIATION

1018   **The Roman System.**

Vowels: *Long*   *Short*

  ā as in *father;*   **a** as in *facility;*

  ē as in *they:*   **e** as in *get;*
    (but without the faint
    i sound at the end);

  ī as in *machine;*   **i** as in *fit;*

  ō as in *no:*   **o** as in *obey;*
    (but without the faint
    u sound at the end);

  ū as in *rule.*   **u** as in *put.*

  y (in borrowed Greek words) like German *ü* or French *u.*

Diphthongs:

  ae like *ai* in *aisle;*   **ei** like *ei* in *feign;*

  oe like *oi* in *foil;*   **eu** like *ew* in *dew;*

  au like *ou* in *out;*   **ui** like *we.*

Consonants:

Most of the consonants are pronounced as in English, but

  c always as in *cat;*   **s** always as in *this;*

  g always as in *gun;*   **su** as in *suave;*

  ngu as in *unguent;*   **t** always as in *tin;*

  qu as in *quit;*   **x** always as in *extra;*

  r always as in *three;*   **z** like *dz* in *adze;*

  j (consonantal *i*) like *y* in *yet;*

  v (consonantal *u*) like *w* in *well;*

  bs and **bt** like English *ps* and *pt.*

> **Note:** Double consonants are both pronounced but without a break, like the *ll* in English *tailless*. Thus:
>
> bel-lum

1019   **The Italian System.**

Vowels:

> In general as in the Roman pronunciation. However, some prefer to give all the vowels the *quality* of long vowels and to pronounce the short vowels more quickly.

Diphthongs:

> As in the Roman pronunciation except:
>
> **ae** and **oe** like the *e* in *they*.

Consonants:

> Most of the consonants are pronounced as in English, but
> **c** before *e, i, ae, oe* like the *ch* in *charity;*
> **ch** before *e* or *i* like *k;*
> **cc** before *e* or *i* like the *tch* in *match;*
> **sc** before *e* or *i* like the *sh* in *she;*
> **g** before *e, i, ae, oe* like the *j* in *just;*
> **gn** like the *ni* in *onion;*
> **gg** before *e* or *i* like the *dj* in *adjust;*
> **gh** before *e* or *i* like the *g* in *game;*
> **gl** before *i* like the *ll* in *million;*
> **h** is silent, but between two vowels it is like English *k;*
> **r** as in *three* (*i. e.*, trilled);
> **t** before *i* and a vowel (except after *s, t, x*) = *ts;*
> **x** (in words beginning *ex-* followed by a vowel, *h,* or *s*) = *gs;* otherwise *ks.*

> **Note:** Double consonants are both pronounced but without a break like the *ll* in English *tailless.*

NOTES ON VERBS

1020 Irregular Imperatives.

$$
\left.\begin{matrix} \text{dīcō} \\ \text{dūcō} \\ \text{faciō} \\ \text{ferō} \end{matrix}\right\} \text{have} \left\{\begin{matrix} \text{dīc} \\ \text{dūc} \\ \text{fac} \\ \text{fer} \end{matrix}\right\} \text{in the second person singular imperative active.}
$$

1021 Irregular Future Participles Active.

orior, orīrī, ortus sum, *4, intr., I arise:*
   oritūrus, a, um

morior, morī, mortuus sum, *3, intr., I die:*
   moritūrus, a, um

nāscor, nāscī, nātus sum, *3, intr., I am born:*
   nāscitūrus, a, um

ruō, ruere, ruī, rutus, *3, intr., I fall, I rush:*
   ruitūrus, a, um

fruor, fruī, fructus sum, *3, intr., I enjoy:*
   fruitūrus, a, um

pariō, parere, peperī, partus, *3, tr., I bring forth:*
   paritūrus, a, um

sonō, sonāre, sonuī, sonitus, *1, intr., I sound:*
   sonātūrus, a, um

secō, secāre, secuī, sectus, *1, tr., I cut:*
   secātūrus, a, um

juvō, juvāre, jūvī, jūtus, *1, tr., I help:*
   juvātūrus, a, um (but: adjūtūrus, a, um)

lavō, lavāre, lāvī, lautus, *1, tr., I wash:*
   lavātūrus, a, um

1022   **Alternate Endings.** The following are common:

-**ēre** for -**ērunt** in the third person plural perfect indicative active.

-**re**   for -**ris**   in the second person singular of all passive forms.

Cicero prefers -**ris** in the present indicative, but -**re** in the future indicative, present subjunctive, imperfect indicative, and imperfect subjunctive.

Shortened Forms.

1023   1. Forms of the perfect tenses are sometimes shortened.

amāstī		amāvistī
dīxtī		dīxistī
amārunt		amāvērunt
amārō		amāverō
amārim	for	amāverim
audīsse		audīvisse
audīssem		audīvissem
dēlērunt		dēlēvērunt
dēlēssem		dēlēvissem, *etc.*

1024   2. Perfect stems in **īv** sometimes drop the **v** and shorten the **i**.

audierat	for	audīverat
petierat		petīverat, *etc.*

1025   **Dō.** The a is short in all forms of **dō, dare, dedī, datus,** *1, tr., give,* except in **dā** (the imperative) and in **dās** (second person singular present indicative active).

INDEX

References are to marginal numbers unless otherwise indicated.

ab (ā), 752, 764, 768, 916, 932-933
abhinc, 923
Ablative, 762-789
  absolute, 912-914
  accompaniment, 772-774
  agent, 764
  cause, 781-784
  comparison, 777-780
  degree of difference, 771
  description, 697-699, 762
  manner, 769
  means, 765
  object, 785, 1010
  place, 915-916
  position of, 466
  price, 788-789
  respect, 770
  separation, 766-768
  time, 920-922, 924
  with adjectives, 766, 775-776
  with prepositions, 932-933, 950-956,
    958-959, 961, 981-983, 986-990, 996-
    998, 1003
about, 938, 946-947, 953
above, 1001-1002
ac (atque), 608-610
  ac sī, 611
Accent, 9-10
accidit, 638, 659
Accompaniment, ablative of, 772-774
according to, 956, 995
Accusative, 745-761
  cognate, 758
  direct object, 745, 1007
  double, 746-754, 1008-1009
  extent of space and time, 761, 919,
    923-924
  in exclamations, 759

  of neuter pronouns and adjectives,
    755-757
  place to which, 917
  predicate, 746, 1009
  specification, 760
  subject of infinitive, 893, 897, 904
  time, 761, 919, 923-924
  with infinitive, 579, 3; 897-904
  with prepositions, 934-949, 957, 960,
    962-980, 984-985, 991-995, 999-
    1002, 1004
ācer, 80, 94-95
across, 1004
Active voice, 144, 160-239, 312-321
ad, 712, 872, 917, 934-938
adeō, 551
Adjective clauses, 615-636, 1017
Adjectives, 72-102, 845-859
  ablative with, 766, 775-776
  agreement, 474-478, 808-811, 865, 888
  attributive, 477-478, 866-867, 869
  comparison, 89-102, 853-855
  dative with, 742-743
  declension, 72-88, 101-102
  demonstrative, 133-137, 464, 794
  genitive with, 687-688, 695, 722-723
  gerundive as, 865-869, 878-884
  infinitive after, 890, 906
  intensive, 138, 808-810
  interrogative, 141, 464, 503, 660
  irregular, 84-88
  of quantity, 112-122, 464, 687, 700-
    701, 705, 755
  participles used as, 309, 907, 911
  position of, 464-465
  possessive, 125, 131-132, 710, 800, 802
  predicate, 474-476, 878, 894, 900, 1006
  relative, 139, 615

References are to marginal numbers unless otherwise indicated.

References are to marginal numbers unless otherwise indicated.

References are to marginal numbers unless otherwise indicated.

References are to marginal numbers unless otherwise indicated.

References are to marginal numbers unless otherwise indicated.

References are to marginal numbers unless otherwise indicated.

References are to marginal numbers unless otherwise indicated.

References are to marginal numbers unless otherwise indicated.

References are to marginal numbers unless otherwise indicated.

References are to marginal numbers unless otherwise indicated.

References are to marginal numbers unless otherwise indicated.

References are to marginal numbers unless otherwise indicated.

References are to marginal numbers unless otherwise indicated.

References are to marginal numbers unless otherwise indicated.

References are to marginal numbers unless otherwise indicated.